HEAVEN'S CURRENCY

Heaven's Currency

INVESTING IN THE
THINGS THAT MATTER MOST

Cos Davis

Heaven's Currency:
Investing in the Things That Matter Most

Published by Family Resource Services
Franklin, Tennessee

ISBN-978-0-578-25664-1

All scripture references are taken from the New American Standard Bible copyright 1960, 1962, 1968, 1971, 1972, 1973 by The Lockman Foundation.

To Cecelia, my faithful wife and friend

Contents

Introduction

What is heaven's currency? Let's take a few minutes to talk about currency and what I mean by this book's title.

Prior to the emergence of money, people bartered for what they wanted or needed. For example, a farmer might trade some of his produce or animals for a plow or tool owned by another farmer. Bartering is not uncommon today. John may say to his friend, "I will help you repair your car if you will help me paint my kitchen." In such an instance, the currency or standard of payment is agreed upon by two individuals.

The use of currency as a form of exchange for goods and services dates back to Mesopotamia, almost five thousand years ago. Today, 249 countries have an official currency or currencies. This currency or money serves as legal tender sanctioned by that country for the payment of debt or services. The United States has the dollar as its medium of exchange; the eurozone countries have the euro; Japan has the yen; and so on. Checks, credit cards, and debit cards are widely used today instead of government-issued currency. The assumption behind the use of these forms of payment is that you have the currency in your bank or financial institution to cover the cost of the purchase.

The check you write or the plastic you use to purchase something is not the currency; it is a substitute for the real thing. You can get into trouble if you do not know the difference. This brings to mind a funny incident that took place with one of my children several years ago. We were at a store, and she was insisting that we buy a certain item she wanted. My response was, "Sweetheart, we don't have the money to buy it." Her solution: "Just write a check."

I didn't have the money in the bank to cover the thing she wanted and take care of other financial obligations. This reality was very much in play in my decision to deny my child what she wanted. One of the hard realities I have learned along the way is this: you shouldn't buy what you can't pay for.

A person's financial wealth in this world is measured by how much of his country's currency he possesses or holdings that can be exchanged for that currency. But there is another world. And this world has only one currency. This other world is heaven.

In this book, *Heaven's Currency*, you will be reminded time and again that you live in two worlds. One world is the temporal existence you have on earth; the other is the eternal world in which you exist at the same time. If you are a Christian, you have dual citizenship. And each world to which you belong has a currency of exchange. You must never confuse or substitute this world's currency for that of the eternal world. This world worships wealth. The other world worships God. And God has determined the currency of his kingdom.

The currency of this world is money or riches. What is the currency of heaven? The currency of heaven is what has bought you and me. Heaven's currency is not material; it is quality of character. It is a disposition, a commitment to seek the well-being of others. It is what motivates every act of goodness and kindness for those in need. In 1 John 4:8, we are reminded of the character of God: "God is love." Jesus said in John 3:16, "For God so loved the world that he gave his only begotten son that whoever believes in Him should not perish but have eternal life." Love is heaven's currency.

This world values money and riches more than anything else. Heaven has a different standard. Heaven exalts love as the greatest treasure. Love has paid the price for us. Love has made the sacrifice to bring us to the Father. Paul reminds the Corinthians of this fact in 1 Corinthians 6:20 and 7:23: "You have been bought with a price." Heaven's currency has bought us and freed us from the power and penalty of sin. We are told in 1 Peter 1:18–19 that heaven's currency has done for us what earth's money can never do: "You were not redeemed with perishable things like silver and gold...but with the precious blood...the blood of Jesus."

If you have committed your life to Christ, you have committed to the currency of his kingdom. Loving God, yourself, and others is your first priority—how you are to spend your life in this world. Love is to be the motivation of how you invest this world's currency, your time and energies.

In the pages ahead, you will be challenged to think about what motivates your choices and to make decisions that will put you on a path to invest your life in those things that matter most. May the return on your investment be great!

PART ONE

Becoming a Savvy Investor

CHAPTER ONE

Responding to Trying Times

Everyone who hears these words of mine and acts upon them may be compared to a wise man who built his house on the rock. And the rain descended, and the winds blew and burst against that house; and yet it did not fall, for it had been founded upon the rock.
—Matthew 7:24–25

Life can be downright difficult at times. The question is not whether we will face hard times and trials but how we will respond to the challenges life throws at us.

Life's routines can be taken from you in a moment without guarantee that it will ever be "normal" again. That being said, it's not all that bad. Perhaps some of the so-called "normal" needed to be challenged or even eliminated.

At the height of the COVID-19 pandemic in 2021, I conducted a survey to gauge how some folks were dealing with COVID-19 and other life events. Jerry, a single, retired engineer, offered the above comment about different crises he has faced over the last few years. Although his routine of volunteerism and family gatherings was drastically altered by the pandemic, you can sense a bit of optimism in his words.

An accident, a sudden illness or death, the loss of a job, the birth of a child, bankruptcy, an unexpected windfall—these can upset the routines of our life. Some people seem to have more than their share of troubles but bear it well, while others are crushed by lesser issues. Life is difficult, but there is a reason for optimism!

Our Life in Review

The convergence of several crises such as we have dealt with in recent years can create a sense of upheaval and bewilderment. At the beginning of this century's third decade, America's economy was booming. Unemployment rates were low—the lowest ever in several minority sectors. The usual political rancor and vindictive rhetoric of Washington, DC, continued to dominate the media in anticipation of November's national elections. But despite the deep political and value-based divisions, our country seemed to be doing pretty well. Most of us had no clue what was about to hit us.

A SARS virus, commonly called COVID-19, discovered in late 2019 in China, made its way to the United States and almost 180 other countries by early 2020. Confusion reigned concerning the virus's strength, how it spread, and the steps needed to mitigate its potential effects. Responses made at the national and some state and local levels were considered by many as overreactions that inflicted death on many elderly people, caused unnecessary damage to the economy, and interrupted our children's education. Children were forced to undergo remote learning for months without seeing their classmates or the inside of a classroom. Life as we knew it was drastically altered by lockdowns imposed by governors, mayors, school administrators, and teachers' unions.

Predictions about the effect of the loss of in-class learning on this future generation are pretty grim. And what will be the lasting impact on our nation's economy and our national psyche going forward? Will these events leave emotional scars and fears similar to the generation who lived through the Great Depression of the 1930s?

While COVID-19 dominated daily news, other devastating events were also hammering us. Thousands of acres of California and the Northwest went up in flames. In 2020, an unprecedented ten hurricanes hit our country's mainland; lives were lost, properties destroyed by floods and raging winds.

While we were dealing with the personal challenges related to the virus and the forces of nature, the long-term, internal battle for our nation's identity continued. For many years, there has been a constant tearing and stretching of the fabric of our country's soul by political rancor in DC, racial tensions, and the counterculture movement.

You may have been among the multitudes who hoped the arrival of January 1, 2021, would somehow usher in a sense of optimism and healing, a cessation of our troubles, and a return to normalcy. What happened? Almost miraculously, vaccines to combat the virus were available by January 2021, but the process of getting people inoculated was cumbersome and disorganized in many states and communities. It would be several months before the medicines would be available to all who needed them.

As the summer of 2021 arrived, and several states began to reopen, there were enough vaccines available for every American citizen, but a large part of the population was unwilling to take them. This reaction was due partly to the growing distrust of the national health leaders and the belief by many that the COVID-19 issue had become politically weaponized.

February 2021 brought a winter storm that paralyzed much of the nation with ice and snow. Wind turbines, which areas like Dallas depended on for electricity, were knocked out of service, leaving hundreds of thousands without heat or water in single-digit temperatures. Many lives were lost, and property damages reached into the billions.

While it is painful to look back at these personal and national tragedies, we must learn from them and move ahead. Will our nation become more united as a result of our shared suffering? Will you and I learn vital lessons and grow from our experiences?

In the fall of 2021, the Johns Hopkins Coronavirus Resource Center estimated the count for American lives lost due to COVID-19 to be in excess of seven hundred thousand, almost five million worldwide. Events such as these serve to remind us that we are often on the thin edge between life and death. The pandemic and other crises underscore how unpredictable life can be. Many who were fortunate enough to survive the staggering assaults of 2020 and beyond may never fully recover from the financial toll exacted on them. Even more tragic were the losses of irreplaceable lives of loved ones who succumbed to the virus and other devastations.

Responding to Past and Future Crises

Crises are nothing new to our country. We have been through tough times before. A 2016 *TIME* magazine article reminds us we have had at least three major national crises in addition to the National Division (1970 through the present) we are currently experiencing.[1] An update of the article would surely add our recent experience to the list. If so, the new list will look like this: the Revolutionary War (1774–1783), the War Between the States (1861–1865), the Great Depression (1929–1938?), the National Division (1970–present), and COVID-19 (2020).

The title of the article referenced above is "How Today's American Crisis Is Different." The article's focus is how, from the 1970s until today, there has been a fracturing, a tearing apart, of the sense of unity and purpose that helped us overcome the earlier crises. E pluribus unum ("Out of many, one") doesn't appear to be working out for us. Political gridlock and polarization define national politics. Where is our great unifying purpose? The Constitution and government that survived the former crises are under serious threat. How long can our nation survive conditions like this?

One of the challenges we have about learning from our problems is the forgetful mindset we have adopted because of the instant news cycle we have become accustomed to. We are bombarded with multiple tragedies, murders, scandals, and wars in real time from home and across the world. Crises are part of the daily news diet, and we simply cannot digest it all. We tend to become hardened to it and develop a survival attitude, reluctant to ponder the profound life lessons crises may hold for us.

How can we look at these enormous challenges from a more personal, optimistic, and faith-based perspective? In his book *Faithful Change*, Dr. James Fowler says that each generation has felt they lived in unprecedented times, experiencing the full range of challenges of human living. To live faithfully, we must learn to make good choices in light of those challenges. Fowler discusses three types of change we must negotiate if we are to live faithfully: (1) developmental change, (2) healing or reconstructive change, and (3) change due to disruptions and modifications of the systems that shape our lives.[2]

Developmental change is the process of physical, emotional, and intellectual challenges we face in our life cycle. We begin with conception and continue to change through birth, young childhood, preadolescence, teenager, young adult, and so on until old age and death. We continue this process as we deal with the two additional areas of challenge.

The second area, which Fowler refers to as "healing or reconstructive change," has to do with the need for healing from harmful patterns of emotion and thinking that we have adopted to help us feel safe and less vulnerable to the realities of life. This false sense of self and security is challenged when we lose a job, face a major health crisis, lose a loved one, or go through a divorce or other significant disruption. Such a crisis presents an opportunity to reassess who we are and to make necessary changes.

Change due to systems that shape our lives has to do with the challenges that come from our participation in our society's social, political, and economic processes. We often feel the only control we have in these areas is how we will respond to the decisions of those in power. We are currently in the midst of what is often labeled as a cultural war. One of the challenges a believer faces in this postmodern culture is how to maintain a faithful, loving witness in a society we believe to be in a rapid downward spiral. While we don't control many of the financial, health-related, and political issues that affect us, we must learn from these crises and allow love to motivate our choices.

Life often poses a variety of challenges, coming at us from various directions. To live well, we must understand how our everyday choices create patterns of decision making that will ultimately prove to be wise or foolish when the next crisis comes. And troubles will come to each of us in one form or another.

Sadly, lots of folks may look back on these crisis events and regret their lack of preparation for the problems they faced. Some will wish they had spent more time with those they have lost. Others will chide their lack of financial discipline and regret they didn't put away some savings for times like these.

Those most fortunate are those who will come to terms with the fact that material possessions and money, while necessary, are not a reliable source for our security. We are made for another world, and it is to our great benefit that we invest our life and temporal possessions in what matters most to God.

Whether solely personal or shared with much of humanity, every crisis is an opportunity to reassess how you live and invest in God's priorities. There are more crises ahead, and the daily investments you make will be crucial in weathering the coming storms.

Many believe our nation is in a great crisis politically, economically, and morally. Are the vitriol and divisiveness harbingers of a country that is about to come apart at the seams? Where is that something or someone to bring us together, to unite us?

A Story of Hope

Our national need for unity and purpose is analogous to that of each of us. Just as our nation must have a unifying purpose to survive, you cannot personally survive crisis after crisis if you are divided about life's meaning within yourself.

The following is another response to the survey I mentioned earlier. I had emailed Brian to ask if I could call him to discuss the possibility of him doing the survey. Brian and I had met through his work with the Cystic Fibrosis Foundation and had established a cordial relationship. I was aware of the unspeakable tragedy he and Janet had suffered years ago when their eighteen-year-old, Skylar, had taken her life. As it happened, the morning I called was the eleventh anniversary of Skylar's death. I listened to his lingering grief, and we later talked about the survey. A few days later, I received his work.

There were three questions to the survey: (1) one about the crises events he and his family have dealt with over the past several years, (2) another to assess how he believed he is doing emotionally, spiritually, and physically in relation to the crises he identified, and (3) the role his faith has played in dealing with his crises.

During the years since Skylar's death, Brian lost his younger sister and both parents. About three years ago, Brian began a more challenging job with his company, one requiring travel and coordination with fifteen offices in eight states. Like countless Americans have experienced, COVID-19 has limited his ability to do a job that requires a good deal of personal contact and team building.

Following are some of the insights into how Brian has dealt with the tremendous losses and challenges he has faced in his own words:

> I don't want anyone else to have to lose a child, and I work hard to make sure that doesn't happen. It has given me a personal insight and perspective on talking with parents who have lost a child. I am in the same "club" with them, and it is not one you volunteer to be part of.

> I was not as prepared for the storms as I am now. Jesus is the Storm Calmer. Our only hope of surviving is having Jesus and some great friends in our boat with us. I have discovered how important having friends who have your back really is so important. Whatever storms you are going through will not define you, destroy you, or be your destiny. Most importantly, don't let it define you!

There are parts of Brian's experience that resonate with me. Perhaps you also know something of the devastating anguish, heartbreak, and frustration he has experienced. Brian has made some very wise choices and was able to turn his grief and loss into a passion for helping others.

When you think about what you have been through, don't you want to learn how to make the wisest choices possible? My purpose in writing this book is to challenge you to see and live life in a way you may have never done before. I want you to make a paradigm shift in the way you think about the meaning of life and do something about how you live before it's too late.

Heaven's Currency is my invitation to consider how you can invest your life in a way that prepares for life's major crises and the ultimate crisis of your death. You have been created and redeemed to use God's love—heaven's currency—to help heal and restore a broken world. Consequently, this book will challenge you to consider the practical implications of what it means to love as God loves in this time and place in which you live.

I firmly believe our ability to endure and grow through life's storms depends on how we choose to invest our life. This idea of our life as an investment is carried through the four major sections of the book. You will begin with "Becoming a Savvy Investor." From there, you will move to the challenge of "Investing to Maximize Your ROI." Part three will focus on some very personal aspects of how you can use heaven's currency as you explore "Extraordinary Investment Opportunities." The closing part of the book is a reminder that there are great rewards for living in obedience to God's will. "Return on Your Investment" will be an encouraging finish to your venture in this book.

An exercise called an Investment Review comes at the close of each chapter. The reviews are designed to help you think more deeply about how you can apply what you have read. It's time now to look at the first Investment Review.

INVESTMENT REVIEW

1. What do you think is currently our nation's greatest crisis?

2. What are some ideas you may have to begin to address this crisis?

3. Where do you see yourself in relation to Dr. James Fowler's suggestions on how to live faithfully regarding the three areas of adjustments we need to make?

4. In what ways do you identify with the loss and hope in Brian's story?

CHAPTER TWO

Five Truths That Can Change Your Life

You shall know the truth and the truth shall make you free.
—John 8:32

"What is truth?" This was the skeptical question Pontius Pilate raised when Jesus claimed his earthly mission was all about truth: "For this I have been born, and for this I have come into the world, to bear witness of the truth" (John 18:37). Truth didn't matter to Pilate. Although he believed Jesus to be innocent of the charges against him, he chose the politically expedient path. Later that morning, Jesus was crucified.

Likewise, the truth was a threat to those who wanted to silence Jesus. They were drunk on power, and Jesus's life and teaching were exposing the shabby lies of their pretentious religion. These religious leaders would fabricate any lie, go to any length, to get him out of the way. The crucifixion appeared to settle the issue. They had won—or so they thought. There was just one big problem: you may silence truth for a while, but you can't kill it.

Jesus said, "I am the way, and the truth and the life" (John 14:6). Our Christian faith rests on the truth, the reality that God raised Jesus from the dead. There is such a thing as absolute truth. And in this chapter, I want to share five of those truths that can change your life.

Before investigating these life-changing truths, I want to remind you of an essential fact about truth—any truth. Truth has the power to change your life, but you must do something for that to happen.

In the early 1880s, Thomas Edison developed a way to provide electricity to areas of New York City. For centuries experiments had been conducted with lightning, but few saw the practical potential for harnessing the power of electricity for everyday use. There were some early doubters about its effectiveness, but today electricity has become so widespread that no one wants to do without the cool air it can produce on a humid day or the many other conveniences it makes possible.

Electricity is a reality, a kind of "truth," if you will. Electricity can dispel the darkness from a room, but that will happen only if you do what is necessary to release its power. Likewise, these five truths can change your life. What will you need to do for that to happen? Believe them to the extent that you put them into practice. When Jesus said, "You shall know the truth and the truth shall set you free," he was talking about knowing truth at a deep, experiential level. This kind of knowing requires action, putting the idea into use.

Please read closely and internalize these truths because they will provide a greater understanding of what is to come. Truth really matters to you only if you allow it to change the way you think and act upon it. To achieve the effect I think these truths deserve, please read each statement aloud a couple of times before studying the explanation that follows it. Ready? Here we go with the first truth.

Truth One: God Loves You and Has a Plan for Your Life
What's your response to this statement? If you've grown up going to church or have been raised in a Christian home, this is something you have heard for a long time. Maybe it's one of those ideas you've heard so many times you don't think about it much anymore. But you and I need to think about it! We need to think deeply about it because understanding that God, the Creator of this universe, loves us is critical to living a purposeful and fulfilling life.

Why do I say believing this truth is so important? Jesus tells us in John 3:16 that God loves us. We should take Jesus at his word, but why is it important to believe this? When you know someone loves you, you trust them to always try to do what is best for you. That kind of love between a man and woman is a wonderful thing. That kind of love helps our children feel secure and trust us even when they don't like our decisions. Now think about what being loved by God implies. Knowing I am loved by God means I can trust the events of my daily life and my future to his wisdom. This kind of security bolsters my faith in him when times are tough. In those times, I know he is working in everything for good for me (Rom. 8:28). Being confident that God loves me gives me hope in difficult times and encourages me to live obediently under his care.

Our loving Father also has a plan for our lives. I'm not thinking specifically about the work or profession we will have on earth. God certainly can and will lead us in our vocational choices, but God has a greater plan than that for us! This plan is for you, me, and everyone who confesses faith in Jesus as our Savior. If you think Jesus died on the cross and rose again to just save you from hell, you need to listen up. Yes, if you truly trust in Jesus, you will go to heaven, but God has a plan for you between the time he saved you and the time you die. Specifically, his plan is to make a new person out of you. He's not going to leave you alone. He wants to change the way you think and the way you treat him, yourself, and others. He wants to continue the change he began in you when you first trusted him. And where is this plan leading? He wants to make you like Jesus. You can read it for yourself in Romans 8:29.

This truth is central to the Christian worldview. God has created you in his image and has a plan to save you from your sin, pride, and selfishness. This plan, often referred to by terms such as *salvation* and *sanctification*, is initiated and brought about as his Spirit awakens you to God's love and forgiveness provided through the cross and resurrection of Jesus. Once you have responded in faith to God's offer of eternal life through the work of Jesus, he goes about the process of accomplishing his ultimate purpose for you: to form in you the very character of Jesus.

That's right. God's master plan is to use your life experiences, the good and the difficult, to form the character of Jesus in you. His plan is for you to live a surrendered, obedient life in which you live in the power of his Spirit and consciously, proactively dedicate and use your time, money, energies, and talents to serve him and others.

Our society is experiencing a drift away from absolute truth, the idea that some things are valid for all people. The Bible contains some absolutes, and we do not get to determine what is true based on our opinion or what suits the particular lifestyle we want to live. One of those absolutes is that your life is a time-sensitive trust from God. Now let's explore this important truth.

Truth Two: Your Life Is a Time-Sensitive Trust from God

Does truth really matter to you? If it does, there are several things you will need to do in order to have the truth and use it well. First, you will need a trustworthy source. Where will you get the information by which you will make decisions? This is an area of deep concern to me because I recognize two things about human nature. First, even well-intentioned people don't have all the facts about most things. We make interpretations about things we see and hear according to the way we see life. We rarely know all the facts and circumstances as to why someone does something we don't agree with. Do you think that may be why Jesus tells us not to judge others?

The second thing I have learned through many difficult experiences is that some people make a habit of lying. I used to think that something I read was true because it was in print or because someone in a place of leadership said it. How naive and gullible I was. No longer am I that silly and ignorant. We have people and movements in our country who have agendas that will basically destroy our country. Jesus dealt with people like this all the time. He knew who they worked for and what they represented. We cannot hide from the fact that our country is under attack. Ignoring problems doesn't make them go away.

So what are we to do? Find reliable sources of information. How do you know they are reliable? Does what they say or write agree with common sense? Is there a consistency in what they say and what they do? Is their basic message supported by scriptural teachings and principles?

The bottom line for me is this: Does what I am reading or being told pass the tests of scriptural truth and common sense? Now let's see if the following idea will meet these tests.

The second life-changing truth I want you to consider is that *your life is a time-sensitive trust from God.*

This truth is prominent in the teachings of Christianity. Biblical concepts such as stewardship, responsibility, judgment, rewards, discipleship, and Christ's lordship rest on the premise that we have been entrusted with something. A trust is a property or interest held by one person for the profit or benefit of another. The owner of the property or interest, in this case, is God, your Creator. You are the trustee or steward of this trust.

What is it that God has entrusted to you? He has entrusted you with your life and all that comes with it. You belong to Him. Your body, wealth, gifts, talents, and time belong to Him. And according to scriptural teachings such as the Parable of the Talents, you are accountable for how you manage his interests. Even a cursory reading of this story in Matthew 25:14–30 will dispel any doubt or misunderstanding about God's expectation and judgment related to the life he has given us.

What is the time limit on the trust God has given you? The trust remains in effect until you die. During your lifetime, you are allowed to make choices that determine your character and your ultimate destiny in heaven or hell. You are not guaranteed a specific amount of time in which to execute your trust. Scripture and common sense caution you not to presume you have another day past the one you are now living. You do not know when the time for your trust will run out.

Do you believe this truth about your life being a time-sensitive trust from God? What are you willing to do to change in order to take it seriously? How will you treat God, yourself, and others in light of this truth? God gives us only one day at a time, and that is all we have. Yesterday is gone. Tomorrow may not come for us, but we have now. Let's give God and others our best today, and every day he may give us.

Truth Three: You Live in a Two-World Marketplace in Which You Invest Every Day

We live in two worlds simultaneously: our current physical existence and the spiritual realm that is every bit as real as the trees, houses, and people around us. Both worlds have a marketplace with something to "sell" us. And every day, we make choices to invest our time, money, and energies in what one or both of these markets have to offer.

This idea may seem a bit odd to you, but think about it for a moment. A physical marketplace is a location or virtual site where you buy something such as tires for your car or a meal with your family. An exchange occurs when you use a plastic card representing payment or pay by cash or check. You are provided with a set of tires or a good meal with your family for your investment. Money is the currency of the physical marketplace.

On the other hand, the spiritual marketplace (heaven) offers abundant life in the here and now *and* the promise of eternal life through a personal relationship with God. The spiritual life is about investing in the relationships that matter most in life. Our life, given in love, is the currency we have to invest in the things that matter most to us.

Every day you and I invest in those things that pertain to our life: time, money, words, talents, and energies. Each day you invest twenty-four hours in work, sleep, and various other kinds of activities. You use the money you have earned to support the people and things you value. You give your talents to help others in organizations you deem important and use your words and energies to promote values at the core of your being.

What are you getting from these transactions? You are getting the things you believe you want or need. If your interest is pleasure and what you can see, taste, feel, and take from life before you die, that is how you will invest your life. Likewise, if you believe your life is a gift from God to be used for his glory, you will choose to invest your life in developing personal character and faithful relationships. In both instances, you choose how you invest with the hope of getting a return on your investment.

The idea that life is a marketplace in which you invest every day is solidly biblical. The concept is directly expressed or implied in many of Jesus's teachings (e.g., the Parable of the Talents, the Sermon on the Mount, and so forth). Those who embrace Christianity believe life has a purpose and that we are accountable to our Creator for how we use our lives. If the Bible is true, we should be concerned with how we invest our time, money, talents, and energies.

Therefore, do not throw away your confidence, which has great reward. For you have need of endurance, so that when you have done the will of God, you may receive what was promised.
—Hebrews 10:35–36

You live in a two-world marketplace with two fundamental choices: to live by God's plan or go it on your own. This choice is the most consequential one a human being is ever called on to make. But choose you must. Our choices have attendant consequences; this one determines the direction of the brief life you have on earth and your eternal destiny. How will you invest your life today?

Truth Four: Your Investment Choices Determine Your Character, Which In Turn Determines Your Future

The way we use time and money indicates what is most important to us. Your behaviors related to these two resources give a vital clue about your most deeply held values. Your character, your religion, is not what you profess to believe but how you live. The decisions you make concerning your resources are the real test of who you are, not who you think or say you are. Day after day, you make choices that, little by little, make you more like Jesus or put you further and further away from being the person you were created to be.

Your incredible power of choice is exercised in many ways every day by how you treat God, yourself, family members, and others. Since your character is always in the process of developing or devolving, it is critical that you understand and cooperate with God's plan and make wise choices in the way you invest your time, money, and energies. Now...on to truth number five.

Truth Five: Following God's Plan Will Bring Great Rewards in This Life and the One to Come

One of my favorite movies is *Secondhand Lions*, the story of two elderly brothers who retire to an old house on a run-down farm in a rural area in the Southwest. They acquired great wealth in their adventures in the Middle East and hid it in their dilapidated barn. Although they were elderly, they had not lost their zeal for adventure and were willing to go to their stash to support whatever might interest them. They flew a biplane, bought a yacht for their small lake and a skeet machine for their entertainment, and a secondhand lion they proposed to hunt for sport.

One of the brothers decided to plant a vegetable garden to occupy their time and provide healthy food for their meals. He bought packets of seeds, supposing them to be a variety of vegetables such as carrots, cucumbers, squash, corn, and so forth and put the package at the head of each row to identify the vegetable they would gather from the seeds planted there. One day while working in the garden, one brother looks over the expanse of the growing plants and asks, "What is this?" and repeats the question about various other rows. The brother whose idea it was to plant the garden answers, "Well, this is squash, that is carrots, and this one is corn," to which the inquiring brother replies, "It all looks the same to me; it's all corn." He throws down his hoe and storms out of the cornfield. Although the packaging was labeled as carrots, squash, and assorted other vegetables, it was all corn. The truth was in the seed, not what the package advertised it to be.

There is a consistent biblical theme that we must not ignore: we will reap what we have planted or sown. We may be fooled by the packaging, but the seed determines what will be produced. Corn seed grows corn, no matter what the package says it is. The world and its marketplace advertise products and ideas that appeal to our pride, comfort, self-indulgence, and ego. Christ appeals to making a godly character that rewards us with a deep peace and purpose in this life and great rewards in the life to come. The biblical message is unmistakable: there are two paths in life. One leads to personal destruction, the other to eternal life. Sin, rejection of God's will, brings death. Obedience to God's will brings life. That eternal life becomes yours the moment you choose to respond by faith to Christ's claim as your Lord and Savior.

It's Your Decision

You may disagree with my conclusions, but I ask you to invest the time to look at the possibility I am correct. Caution: the five truths will challenge you to live by principles that can realign your priorities and change the entire direction of your life.

You are putting your time, energy, and financial resources into something. You are investing. But are you being smart with your investments?

This book is about investing. More specifically, it is about the most important investment you will ever make. You have one life to live. You will use your time, money, energy, and talents in various kinds of endeavors. Then you will die. My question is this: What difference will it make that you lived? Hopefully, you will gain the great rewards that come to you every day from following Jesus and come to the end of your life with some incredible rewards waiting for you in heaven. Embracing these five truths will secure that hope for you.

INVESTMENT REVIEW

1. What major life or family events have you experienced over the past three to five years?

2. Describe where you believe you are today emotionally, spiritually, and physically.

3. Review the five truths and list specific ways these spiritual truths helped you deal with challenges you have faced.

4. How can the five truths guide you to live at your best in future challenges?

CHAPTER THREE

Two Worlds

Do not be conformed to this world, but be transformed
by the renewing of your mind...
—Romans 12:2

Are you a savvy investor? When you need a set of tires or a new appliance, do you investigate product ratings to be sure you get the best bang for your buck? Do you attempt to negotiate the asking price? If you do these things, you probably have a pretty good understanding of how our capitalistic economic system works. It is a supply/demand economy in which a supplier sells a product to retailers or wholesalers who, in turn, sell to you. In our system, everyone is a buyer.

Several years ago, I wanted to replace the radio on an older car, and the only one I could find was at an auto salvage shop in another town. I was happy when I located the part, and the owner was happy to see me. However, he was not in a negotiating mood. His reply to my request to lower what I thought to be an inflated price went something like this: "Sir, I have the part you need, and that's the price you'll have to pay if you want it." That was supply and demand in action. I swallowed deeply, pulled out my wallet, and handed over the cash. He supplied the part, and I invested the money. That is capitalism in real life.

The Lure of the Marketplace

I am a Christian and a capitalist. I am very grateful for the opportunities and standard of living I enjoy today because of capitalism. I believe the capitalistic economic system is the best this world has to offer, but I am aware that I must carefully choose between whether some of its offerings are ends in themselves or means to a greater end. I must worship God, not worship at the altar of capitalism.

Advertising is the mainstay for letting us know what we can buy. It is so pervasive that we hardly notice the subtle seduction in this system anymore. It is in the very air we breathe. The noise and the unrelenting call of the marketplace world have become so commonplace and addictive that a few moments of silence or solitude prompts us to reach for some gadget to calm us.

Ours is a very alluring culture, and we must be alert to the fact that there are forces that want to use whatever instruments or means to distract us from God's plan for our lives. To ignore this fact can lead us to make investments of our time, money, and energies to promote and support values and principles directly opposed to those taught and lived out by our Lord.

The marketplace of things and ideas calls us hour after hour, day after day. Our phones, print media, TVs, radios, and other gadgets are the instruments of the marketplace's clamoring. It is our world, our life of getting and spending. We feel at home here—at least, some part of us does.

But don't be naive about this marketplace. If you think the market is only about getting you to buy things—furniture, appliances, automobiles, beer, et cetera, et cetera, et cetera—you haven't been paying much attention to the subtle or underlying messages of the product promoters. No, the appeal is to more than real needs. Marketers often attempt to create a perceived need to persuade us that our value will be upgraded by having what they have to sell. They tell us we are smart or cool or sexy or successful or like our favorite actor or athlete if we will only buy this product. And they even imply that by investing in their product we could be happy. What a great deal!

As believers, we need to face the hard, cold facts. Things don't make us happy. The marketplace is after our money, and some parts of it are after us—to directly or indirectly influence our thinking about what is essential in life.

They Want More Than Our Money
The world in which we invest our lives has many salespersons beyond the supermarkets or other places or venues. Who are some of the marketers? They are politicians who make laws, teachers in our local schools and universities, religious leaders, entertainers from the music and movie industries, not-for-profits, news organizations, social media, and TV and radio talk-show hosts. These people are daily influencing our culture with their values. If we listen to and "buy" just anything our culture is selling without critical evaluation, we may become more a reflection of current values than those consistent with the teachings of Christ. We must learn how to be smart investors in the "two-world" marketplace in which we live.

In his monumental work *The 7 Habits of Highly Effective People*, Stephen Covey has observed that much of the so-called "success literature" of the early part of the twentieth century was very shallow and "superficial." He describes what he found this way: "It was filled with social image consciousness, techniques, and quick fixes—with social band-aids and aspirin that addressed acute problems and sometimes even appeared to solve them temporarily, but left the underlying chronic problems untouched to fester and resurface time and again."[1]

Covey's research revealed that in the 150 years before this shift toward a more superficial approach, the literature about the foundation for success focused on the "character ethic." This earlier literature emphasized qualities such as "integrity, humility, fidelity, temperance, courage, justice, patience, industry, simplicity, modesty and the Golden Rule."[2]

A simple, quick-fix approach toward the meaning of living a successful life is very much evident in today's world. But while there has been deterioration in values in many areas of business, politics, education, religion, and the entertainment industry, we should not assume this change in cultural mores is something different from what believers of other centuries have confronted. What is different is that technological advances in communication have made the dissemination of value-intrinsic messaging so much easier. High tech is our world, the marketplace in which we live, and we must learn how to be good citizens while remaining faithful to our calling from another kingdom.

The question and follow-up invitation of the ancient prophet Isaiah are just as relevant in today's high-tech world as they were in the agrarian society in which he lived. Times have changed, but the needs of the human heart to find lasting meaning and purpose have not. Consider his timeless wisdom: "Why do you spend money for that which is not bread, and your wages for that which does not satisfy? Listen carefully to me, and eat what is good, and delight yourself in abundance. Incline your ear and come to Me. Listen that you may live..." (Isa. 55:2–3).

Living in Two Worlds

In the sequel to Og Mandino's highly acclaimed *The Greatest Salesman in the World*, Mandino's elderly salesman, Hafid, makes this clear-eyed observation:

> Now I can see that the world is a market where everything is marked at a set price, and I must stand by my decision, whatever I buy with my time, labor, and ingenuity, whether it be riches, ease, fame, integrity or knowledge. I must never act like a child who, when he has purchased one thing, regrets that he does not possess another. Since the daily trades that I make for part of my life are difficult to rescind, let me be certain in the future that I am laying up things of value and permanence for my toil and sweat.[3]

The salesman understood the fundamental truth that many never seem to "get." We live in two worlds. One world is temporal; the other is eternal. One is the world of our earthly existence of labor and interaction, focused on the here and now. The other world—the eternal reality of the kingdom of Christ—calls for absolute loyalty which is demonstrated by obedience to his teachings.

Those who are fortunate enough to live in a democratic republic still enjoy the freedom to practice our faith, even though many of the ethical principles of our faith are under attack. Those who believe in the sanctity of life and sexual modesty are often seen as prudes and as being out of touch with many current cultural mores. These are just two of many conflicts between biblical teachings and the postmodern marketplace in which we live.

The challenge of "being in the world but not of the world" is a long-standing one for Christians. Richard Niebuhr reminds us that "the question of Christianity and civilization is by no means a new one...the problem has been an enduring one through all the Christian centuries."[4]

Two questions seem to follow naturally from what you have just read. *How do I balance my commitment to be faithful to Christ and his teachings and be a good citizen at the same time? What are some practical things I can do with my time, gifts, and resources to have a positive influence on the temporal culture in which I live?* While these are simple questions, working out their practical answers is quite challenging.

Let's begin our quest for grappling with these and other questions with a brief look at two critical aspects of our problem: culture and character. A third critical issue—our capacity to make responsible choices when values of our culture and our faith collide—will be addressed in chapter five.

What Is Culture?

What comes to mind when you think about the term *culture*? Do your thoughts go to the overwhelming complexities of the current culture? Or do you focus on the immediate setting in which you are now living? Culture is broad and narrow at the same time. You live in a small culture that is part of a very large culture. Whatever the case, culture is about ideas, customs, habits, beliefs, social organizations, business and religious organizations, education, technical progress, and values. Our forms of government, philosophies of life, art, science, entertainment, and economic systems are reflections of our culture and marketplace. The bottom line is this: our corporate and personal cultures are intrinsically tied to what we believe. What we do and how we live express our fundamental values, good or bad.[5]

To a large extent, culture is an expression of what the people of that culture value. Many pundits have used the term *divisive* to describe the state of our nation's moral, racial, economic, and political climates. Values, good ones or bad ones, can be influenced and changed over time. We didn't get to where we are overnight. A battle for the soul of our country has been going on for more than a century. Warren Susman, an astute observer of American culture, has opined, "One of the fundamental conflicts…is between two cultures—an older culture, often loosely labeled Puritan-republican, producer-capitalist culture, and a newly emerging culture of abundance…a significant and profound clash between different moral orders. The battle was between rival perceptions of the world, different visions of life."[6]

Susman further states that cultures tend to create an "ideal" for their citizens. The American Dream of homeownership and the lifestyle afforded by a well-paying job is such an ideal. The older culture emphasized character and moral qualities, while the newer culture insisted on personality.[7]

An important part of the culture war is being waged in state and national politics. Progressives see the Constitution as a living document that can be interpreted to meet the changing values of the times. Conservatives believe the Constitution should be interpreted according to the principles the Founding Fathers had in mind when they wrote it. Politicians, news media, and social media platforms have great power to create and disseminate their ideas and promote the values they want to shape our culture. This overlay of political division is an important and challenging aspect of the everyday culture we must somehow navigate.

This ongoing battle over the Constitution and individual rights is about ultimate authority. Is the Constitution a fixed, unchanging authority to guide our nation, or is it obsolete and needing to be updated to reflect a more progressive view of life? Lots of time, money, and energy are being expended to determine the nature of the authority under which we will live.

Think about it: protecting and maintaining our culture is an expensive business. Almost everywhere you go, you see new bridges and roads being built or old ones under repair. Our houses, schools, hospitals, and places of worship are always in need of upkeep or repair. And we must also pay attention to the education and defense needs of our country. On and on it goes. We cannot maintain the "American way of life" without lots of effort.[8]

Within the larger national, state, and local cultures is our personal culture of family and friends. How does the larger culture affect our values and the way we live? Do we seriously think about and weigh the ideas that are trending in the broader culture? Is there an "authority" that stands above all cultures to which we turn for guidance in these confusing times? Learning to think for yourself and developing a foundation of core values contrary to many of the norms accepted in the broader culture is hard work. We will explore more about the family and values in a later section.

Christians are given many warnings in scripture about the danger posed by culture and are counseled to act wisely, giving full allegiance to Christ. The apostle Paul's challenge in Romans 12:2 is such an example: "And do not be conformed to this world, but be transformed by the renewing of your mind, that you may prove what the will of God is, that which is good and acceptable and perfect." The "world" to which Paul refers has a value system it is selling, one that is often at odds with the teachings of Christ. As long as we live, the follower of Christ will contend with the temptation to live in both value systems. Jesus does not afford us that option: "No one can serve two masters; for either he will hate the one and love the other, or he will hold to one and despise the other. You cannot serve God and mammon" (Matt. 6:24).

In his mid-twentieth-century book *The Struggle of the Soul*, Dr. Lewis Sherrill writes of the extraordinary strength of character demanded to thrive in modern civilization:

Modern civilization requires that the individual be
a person of extraordinary strength if he is to thrive
in the midst of that civilization...modern civilization demands character marked by a high degree of
strength and maturity in those who would survive
it...while the civilization is requiring one thing in
the character of men, the society out of which that
civilization has arisen tends to produce the very
opposite in the character of men.[9]

The marketplace or culture in which we live expresses its values about sexual relations, gender identity, material possessions,
political views, and many other areas of life. The culture's effect
in eroding "natural law" has prompted the following observations
by Alex McFarland, founder of Truth for a New Generation: "The
21st century is different from all other generations, at least in this
way: we are living in the first era of an international attempt to
suppress moral knowledge."[10]

The next statement explicitly identifies two areas in which
McFarland sees this erosion of what our nation's founders referred
to as "self-evident truth." "The cultural call to sexual license and
gender fluidity is not the innocuous path to personal freedom our
society is being led to believe. Abandonment of known truth comes
with a painfully high cost."[11]

One of the strongest and most dangerous examples of our culture's lure for the follower of Christ is materialism, the promise that a person can find happiness and meaning in life in the
"American Dream." The notion that a spiritual void can be satisfied
with material things is an ancient lie that attracts many investors.
Materialism's goal in our culture is this: "Your hearts are our goal.
It is your souls we want."

The "world" or culture apart from Christ attempts to provide temporary solutions for the deep hunger inside each of us. We are made in the image of God; we long for meaning and purpose, for a sense of peace and wholeness. Materialism's answer for our soul's need is in sensual pleasures, gadgets, automobiles, houses, money, and fame.

Self-absorption and self-promotion are values marketed in many areas of our culture. Celebrities, politicians, media outlets, athletes, ministers, and ordinary folks: all of us are tempted to create images of ourselves so that others will see us as important. Does this approach to our quest for purpose and meaning suggest an underlying sense of insecurity in who we are deep inside?

Our marketplace does not have an adequate answer for what we need as spiritual beings. This bumper-sticker message expresses the frustration and futility of many who have fallen for our culture's trap about the meaning of life: "If you are not the lead dog, the view never changes."

Churches and Christian organizations are not immune to the value system of our culture. Is the drift to "the left" by several denominational groups on issues such as the sanctity of life, sexual identity, marriage, and family life an indication that the world's value system has replaced biblical revelation? Does such cooperation by these churches and organizations put a religious "stamp of approval" on cultural values contrary to biblical teaching, thus making these practices more acceptable in the minds of many?

Beyond such issues as those just mentioned, we must recognize that religious congregations and organizations have their own culture, a form of government, and leadership. How do they differ from many of the businesses in the communities where they serve? Is there a competitive spirit with other churches? Is there a great sense of pride when comparing buildings and property with that of less affluent congregations? What criteria are used to "call" or employ our church leaders? Where does character rate in comparison to an attractive personality and the ability to effectively communicate? How does the power base or leadership reflect the culture's worship of power and wealth? In *The Law of Rewards*, Randy Alcorn raises such concerns as these and suggests a troublesome issue in the following questions: "Who receives most recognition in many Christian organizations? Who typically serves in places of leadership and determines the direction of ministries? Do we have an abundance of rich fools?"[12]

History has shown that once-great civilizations have failed because they declined in spiritual faith and courage to selfishness, complacency, and apathy and ended in dependency. Civilizations fall because the character or moral standards of many of their citizens are less than honorable. Our Founding Fathers understood that only a people marked by honesty, selflessness, service, and faith in God could maintain the form of government they created.

The marketplace sells what people will buy; otherwise, the sellers go out of business. Some of the alarming issues we face in our current culture result, at least in part, because parents, church leaders, educators, and politicians have bought into lies about what is the end goal of life. Character, or the lack of it, is the underlying problem. We need to return to developing ethical, honest people if we want a better and healthier world for ourselves and the generations to follow.

What Is Character?

Our world is a marketplace of values as well as goods and services. Countless billions of dollars are spent annually by manufacturers, politicians, and the entertainment industry to directly or subtly influence our feelings, thoughts, and actions regarding the ideas or products they have to sell. The imagery on the screen often associates success, power, sexual pleasure, comfort, and physical prowess or well-being with their product. Their product or idea is used to influence values, which in turn influence choice and action.

Once the seller has established brand or idea loyalty with us, we tend to continue to use the product or support the idea we have "bought." Brand loyalty makes shopping and thinking much easier because we tend to keep buying the same product. But it doesn't mean we have made the smartest buy or chosen to live by the wisest idea. Such loyalty can be economically foolish. Likewise, living by foolish values is deadly to our character.

So what is character, and why is it important?

Character is the central issue of life, the prize that is won or lost in the battle always raging between Christ and those cultural values and norms that Satan uses to oppose him. C. S. Lewis makes the case in *The Problem of Pain* that God is not nearly so much concerned with our comfort as he is with our character. God, Lewis contends, allows and uses our pain to get our attention about our character issues: "God whispers to us in our pleasure, speaks in our conscience, but shouts in our pain: it is his megaphone to rouse a deaf world."[13]

What do you think about the idea that facing crises and challenges can make you a godlier person? Let these unsettling words of our Lord's half brother sink in. James 1:2-3 reads this way: "Consider it all joy, my brethren, when you encounter various trials, knowing that the testing of your faith produces endurance. And let endurance have its perfect result, that you may be perfect and complete, lacking in nothing."

I don't like trials and personal challenges. I want life to go smoothly and for everybody to get along. I like peace and consider myself a peacemaker. But stuff happens. The longer I live, the more I am learning that I have no control over much of anything. However, I can choose to be proactive to avoid unnecessary problems and to react wisely to things outside my control. I can also choose to allow God to use my life circumstances and difficulties to improve my character.

Several years ago, I ran across a book titled *The Road Less Traveled*, by psychiatrist M. Scott Peck. Peck begins his book with these sobering words: "Life is difficult." Most people, he argues, are unwilling to deal positively with this fact but moan and groan but never come to terms with that reality. Here is his reasoning:

> Life is a series of problems. Do we want to moan about them or solve them? Do we want to teach our children to solve them?...What makes life difficult is that the process of confronting and solving problems is a painful one...Yet it is in this whole process of meeting and solving problems that life has its meaning.[14]

Further, he implies that our avoidance of life's problems and the suffering that it causes is a primary factor in so much of the anxiety that characterizes our lives and the culture as a whole. He is in agreement with the words of Karl Jung that "neurosis is always a substitute for legitimate suffering."

So what do we say to this? It seems to me we need to be clear minded and make a choice about which of the two world value systems we will embrace. One is the short view. The other is the long view. The short view is stuck in the here and now; the other faithfully strives to live out eternal values in the real world.

Contemporary culture says most moral decisions are relative to what pleases the individual making the decision. The biblical view counters this moral relativism with the position that there are absolute truths that must guide our actions. One set of values promotes fame, wealth, and personality, while the other emphasizes character as the way to get the most out of life.

What are we talking about when we get down to the issue of character?

The *Merriam-Webster Dictionary* defines *character* as "the complex of mental and ethical traits marking a person or group." Following the intent of this statement, we can identify the "character" of a person or group of people by the traits they demonstrate. How do we recognize their traits, apart from the way they act? We cannot.

Several years ago, while doing some postgraduate study in counseling, I formulated my understanding of character this way: "It [character] involves at least three interrelated processes: (1) knowledge/ignorance of ethical standards of behavior, (2) willingness/unwillingness to incorporate the standards into one's life, and (3) practice/lack of practice of the principles in daily living."[15]

The final test of a person's character is whether or not he acts on what is right. To do what is good requires knowledge of what is right as opposed to what is not right.

A person can know what is good or right to do but choose to do differently. In such an instance, the person's actions are inconsistent with what he knows to be good. Such choices indicate a failure of character and show weakness toward compromising one's moral standards in certain situations. Character failure happens when we compromise what we know to be right or good and allow a value such as greed, pride, sexual pleasure, revenge, or some inadequacy linked to some worldly value to influence our actions.

When we have moral lapses, we have a choice to make: to grow or regress in our character development. Those who are wise take responsibility and acknowledge our guilt, repent for our sins, receive forgiveness, and move ahead to gain an understanding of our actions and become more consistent in our character. Others may choose to deny any wrongdoing, blame others, or cover the sin and persist in their destructive behavior. Following this path can eventually desensitize a person to the pangs of conscience to the point where they no longer recognize the difference between good and evil.

As believers, we must understand that we are in the process of developing our character in a culture that often pulls in another direction. Perhaps understanding why our character is important will cause us to pay closer attention to how we act—the real test of what we believe.

Why make an effort to look deeply into your motives and actions when it is so much easier to take the well-worn path of moral laxity? A significant reason is that consistently good character produces the right actions, and consistently good actions build trust. Trust is the single most important ingredient in all functional relationships. Marriages must have a strong foundation of trust to function as they should. Likewise, friendships endure or fail to the degree trust is maintained. Where trust is missing, relationships suffer and die.

While you may recognize some degree of inconsistency between what you say you believe and how you act, you need to stay focused on God's plan for you. If you need a reminder of Christ's teaching concerning the standard for which you are to strive, consider his words in Matthew 22:37: "And He said to him, 'You shall love the Lord your God with all your heart, and with all your soul, and with all your mind.'"

Do you love like this? Do you consistently show your love of God by the way you obey his teachings? Do you love yourself very well? Do you love others and always live unselfishly? Do you recognize your calling as a long, tough road that will require the discipline and hard work involved in surrendering to God?

Jesus's challenge is about God-focused character. The world's focus exalts pride, self-service, deception, and the concepts of "the end justifies the means" and doing or saying whatever it takes to get what you want.

The character Christ wants for us involves knowing and internalizing his teachings and living out their ethical implications in all our relationships. Following Christ is a high and arduous challenge, nothing for the "weak of heart." The bottom line is that your character is expressed by what you do and how you act.

We have taken a brief look at the two-world culture and the values those two worlds exert on our moral character. Next, we will look at "maps," or ways of thinking and acting, that have affected your investments in our two-world system. However, before you go to the next chapter, take a few moments to think about the review questions below.

INVESTMENT REVIEW

1. What is your understanding of the idea that you live in a two-world marketplace?

2. What concerns do you have about the spiritual climate of our culture?

3. What are some of your challenges to developing a God-centered character?

4. What does it mean to "be in the world but not of the world"? What are some things you can do to live faithfully in today's culture?

CHAPTER FOUR

You, the Investor

*Trust in the Lord with all your heart and do not lean on
your own understanding. In all your ways acknowledge
Him, and He will make your paths straight.*
—Proverbs 3:5–6

When making a career change many years ago, I consulted a financial planning professional who had been recommended by a work
colleague. The company I was leaving required me to remove the
funds I had in their 401(k) plan. Knowing very little about how to
make the transfer of funds, I needed someone who specialized in
financial matters. Following my colleague's recommendation has
proven to be a very wise decision.

Within a few years, the first financial expert retired, and my
account went to another well-credentialed financial planner. This
person has earned my trust through good advice tailored to his
understanding of who I am as an investor.

In some of our early conversations, he spent lots of time answering questions and attempting to educate my wife and me about the
market. He showed us a multiyear performance graph and suggested

we "take the long view" in investing. This approach, he explained, would likely minimize risk and give us an acceptable return on our investments. He made it very clear that while some market sectors might earn more, they could also lose more. He worked very hard with us to assess our risk tolerance and to guide us to accomplish our investment goals with as little risk as possible. His advice and guidance have been invaluable in helping me understand myself as an investor. His wisdom has guided me to stay focused on my financial goals and to avoid costly errors. Protecting and leveraging my hard-earned income has been a very rewarding process.

Examining Your Life Maps

As important as sound financial management is, I've come to understand that life is my most valuable asset. Therefore, it is worth my most strenuous effort to understand myself as an investor. The statement attributed to Socrates that "the unexamined life is not worth living" carries a lot of weight with me and deserves careful application. A major tenet of Christianity is that my life has purpose and accountability. If this is true, I must know what "makes me tick" to be able to use my power to choose who I want to be and the direction my life will take.

Perhaps it will help to understand why we invest the way we do by looking into some of the "life maps" that have influenced our choices. I think it is accurate to say that our experiences with many people have shaped us and our view of life. They have influenced how we think about what is important and the very way we live in our two-world marketplace.

You and I have life maps that guide us in the ways we act and react to real-life situations. These ways of viewing life were developed as we experienced our parents and other influencers such as athletes, religious leaders, teachers, peers, and media outlets. These ways of acting are a reflection of our life maps, our perceptions of reality from which we choose to act.

For example, consider how your parents have influenced the development of your "maps." Your parents, like other people in authority, were likely well meaning but sometimes mistaken in the directions they gave and the values they may have taught you. They were not trying to be destructive or mean but were passing along the inadequate maps they had acquired along the way. The following story illustrates how good people in places of authority can mislead us.

In the days before the global positioning system, a businessman had an appointment in an area of town that was unfamiliar to him. After consulting the maps available to him, he decided to take the subway to a point near his destination and finish his trip on foot. He planned carefully to give himself plenty of time. However, in his anxiety about the potential value of the meeting, he accidentally disembarked one stop too early and needed to adjust for his mistake. Taking a deep breath to remain calm, he approached a policeman standing nearby and asked for directions. The friendly policeman assured him he was not far from his destination and could get there without a problem. "Go down the street in front of you for two blocks, and take the first left. Then go three blocks and turn right. You can't miss it," the officer instructed. The man thanked the helpful policeman, looked at his watch, and walked confidently toward his destination.

After the man was out of sight, the policeman realized he had given him the wrong directions. He attempted to follow the man but was called on to help with a traffic jam. The man continued following the policeman's instructions, but after a while, he became very nervous because it was nearly time for his appointment. Feeling pressed for time, he began to run, putting himself farther and farther away from his destination. The result was that, although he got correct directions from another policeman, he was late for the appointment and lost the opportunity represented by the meeting. The moral of the story: Wrong directions, even when sincerely followed, always lead you to someplace other than where you want to be.

Some of us, like the man in the story, follow an inaccurate life map or directions only to end up in the wrong place. Or, to paraphrase something Stephen Covey has said in *The 7 Habits of Highly Effective People*, "They have climbed and climbed, only to find they have put their ladder on the wrong wall."

A Personal Confession

The GPS has replaced the paper map for many of us. I rarely look at a map unless I want to find a place in relation to another area I may be interested in seeing while I am traveling. I have a GPS on my phone and one in my car. The one in my car actually talks to me and generally gives good directions. However, there have been times when it has proven to be inadequate to get me to my exact destination.

When COVID-19 vaccination shots became available in our area in early 2020, my wife and I got signed up. We thought the benefit of getting the shots outweighed the inconvenience of having to go into the large city near us. Although I was generally familiar with the hospital area where we were to get the vaccinations, I plugged the exact information into our GPS, and everything worked just fine—at least, I thought it had. Inside the hospital complex, friendly workers gave good directions to the area for the vaccinations. That accomplished, we headed back to the garage. We didn't realize we were working on inadequate information from the GPS and were lost for over an hour before we found our car. Ever done that?

The "girl with the nice voice" (the GPS) was the problem— good directions to a point but lacking in detail. "Destination is on your left. Destination," she said. I turned left and found what I thought was the south parking garage. When we returned to the garage and attempted to take the elevator to go to our car on the fourth floor, we were totally confused. There was no fourth floor in this garage. We were in the wrong garage. After several failed attempts to find someone to get us to our car, a friendly employee understood our dilemma and called a shuttle to take us to our vehicle.

All this confusion and frustration was due to the fact that the GPS had given inadequate directions. I did exactly as I was instructed. I should have gone one street farther before making the left turn. I did not repeat this error when we returned for our second shot.

On a more serious note, I have made some mistakes because I have followed some wrong maps that I developed from my particular life circumstances. Through reading, counseling, and interacting with wise people and reflecting on scriptural teaching, I have come to realize some of my maps have been inadequate and harmful. For example, I grew up in a family where my hardworking, poorly educated parents lived on credit and got by as economically as possible. While I didn't go without the necessities, I developed the impression that I needed to take care of myself, earn money, and provide for things that my parents could not afford. There were some embarrassing occasions involving a lack of money, the memories of which are easily recalled today. This interpretation affected my spiritual outlook on life and challenged the idea that God would take care of me.

This "map" persisted well into my adulthood. I was overly anxious about money and emotionally concerned about having enough to provide well for my family and any emergencies we might encounter. I was dealing with emotional bondage which had developed from my upbringing and the lie I had believed that I was really on my own.

While an argument could be made that the results of following that map turned out OK, the emotional stress—the anxiety that drove me—was very unhealthy and counter to Jesus's teaching to not be anxious about these things. I was concerned and very anxious because I was following a faulty map. It has taken years to overcome the fear and anxiety this way of thinking produced in my life.

Thankfully, my parents also gave me good maps. They strongly emphasized the need for a good education in order not to repeat their economic struggle. I determined rather early that I would not be trapped in the situation I had experienced at home. I am very grateful for this map my parents attempted to put before me and readily recognize that the four postgraduate degrees and certification in a specialized area I have earned are an expression of the value my parents wanted me to embrace. As I have grown in my faith and understanding of God, I have come to realize that he has been at work in my life and used even the problematic experiences to bless me. He is the Source of everything good that has come to me.

As I have just illustrated, many of our life maps were composed while we were young and trying to find love and approval from our parents. Some values they taught were probably right, while others may not have been so good. If your maps are working well and support the true meaning of life that Christ represents, keep following them. If life is a continuous cycle of mistakes, emptiness, oppression, and bondage, you are following wrong values; it's time to get a new map.

We don't get to choose our family or many of the things that have happened to us. However, we can make new maps because we can choose not to be determined by choices or mistakes other people have made. We can choose how we respond to what has happened or will happen to us. It is critical to acknowledge that we are broken and can become our own worst enemies. Scripture teaches us that God has made us in his image, but we choose to deny the truth and seek our prideful ways. As truth number one says, "God loves you and has a plan for your life." God has the right map for you to follow. The question is: "Do I play God, or do I respond to him in obedience and worship?"

Your Map or God's Plan?

We have a choice about the personal character we develop. Our parents and others who love us can guide us toward ethical values or maps, but we can accept or reject them, follow them, or choose a destructive path. In other words, we are capable of choosing what we will purchase with our time, money, and energy. And being aware of our brokenness should caution us to take the long view before we do something stupid.

What I am getting at is something our culture wants to dismiss, to relegate to the postmodern trash heap of outgrown spiritual ideas. What is it that our world is so slow or unwilling to recognize in the face of unmistakable evidence? We are rebels, lost from God, hopeless apart from his love and looking for meaning in all the wrong places. The prophet Jeremiah's observation gets to the heart of the issue: "The heart is more deceitful than all else and desperately sick: who can understand it?" (Jer. 17:9). This unvarnished truth insults the pride of those who do not want to see or understand the core issue of human existence. We like to think of ourselves as better than that, but God sees us as sinners without hope apart from his mercy and grace to save us from ourselves. One implication of our condition is that sin is attractive to us, and we can easily fall into what is against God and harmful to ourselves and others.

So even if you've had parents and teachers who have given you good maps, you must deal with your soul, your inner self. Do you agree with God about who he says you are and accept the forgiveness provided through the death, burial, and resurrection of Christ? Do you choose to be an obedient follower who lives out his life through the power of Christ, or do you chart your course? To surrender your life to Christ or to "do your own thing" is the single most important choice a human being will ever make. This decision will affect the choices you make regarding the values by which you will live and will have both temporal and eternal consequences.

While having some degree of financial security is a worthy goal, it is not nearly as important as having spiritual security. The psalmist reminds us of the temporal nature of things we possess: "Their inner thought is that their houses are forever. And their dwelling places to all generations; they call their lands after their own names. But man in his pomp will not endure; he is like the beasts that perish" (Ps. 49:11–12).

The psalmist is clearly warning us to keep perspective about what is temporal and what is eternal, that which we must give up at death and that which will endure death. Jesus speaks even more pointedly about the issue of choosing eternal values over the temporal: "Do not lay up for yourselves treasures on earth, where moth and rust destroy, and where thieves break in and steal. But lay up for yourself treasures in heaven, where neither moth nor rust destroys, and where thieves do not break in and steal" (Matt. 6:19–20).

In another place, Jesus raises a question that cautions us to make choices that put our soul's best interest above temporary gain, even if that temporary gain is to possess the whole world and its wealth: "For what will a man be profited, if he gains the whole world and forfeits his soul? Or what will a man give in exchange for his soul?" (Matt. 16:26).

Need a New Map?

What's my point? The bottom-line issue concerns something I mentioned earlier: your view of life and your willingness to risk based on those values. Life has all kinds of risks. Some insist on always playing it safe and choose to protect themselves from friendships, marriage, and anything that would compromise their perceived safety. They risk little and gain little. They choose the temporal over the eternal, this world's marketplace over God. They are unwilling to take the risk of trusting God to do what he promises he will do. Instead, they choose to live by the once-famous line of one of Frank Sinatra's songs, "I did it my way." We choose the way we live based on the way we think about life.

Noted theologian Francis Schaeffer's view on the tremendous impact our thinking has on the way we live is worth serious consideration:

> "As a man thinketh, so is he," is really most profound. An individual is not just the product of the forces around him. He has a mind, an inner world. Then, having thought, a person can bring forth actions into the external world and thus influence it... The inner thought world determines the outward action.[1]

Each of us needs to think clearly about the purpose of life and understand there is a risk involved in whatever decision we make about the value system we choose. Jesus teaches that those who put their trust in the here-and-now world and ignore the deeper spiritual realities of the eternal world will lose everything—their possessions as well as their souls. A person's choice to live only for the temporal world dismisses the gospel as meaningless. This is a statement of faith that life has no real purpose beyond the grave and that whatever sins they have committed have no consequences beyond this life. The life, death, and resurrection of Jesus Christ have no relevance for their life—at least, they are betting their souls on that way of thinking.

Not for the Half-Hearted

Just be clear-minded about this one thing: you do have faith, and that trust is in something or someone. You cannot be a half-hearted follower of Christ and a half-hearted believer in the cultural values that are opposed to him. You cannot have it both ways, with a foot in each world. Christ will have no rival. Either you serve him only, or you do not.

In light of what I have just said, I want you to think about this. The liar Satan is behind the inaccurate and destructive "maps" and the value system of this world that tempt us to want to live in both marketplaces. If you have accepted Jesus as your Savior, Satan cannot steal your salvation from you, but he can and will hinder you from growing and enjoying the life Christ has purchased for you. He and his demons want nothing more than to cause you to fail and to become an ineffective representative for the Lord.

Neil Anderson's book *The Bondage Breaker* offers excellent detail on how Christ is the "bondage breaker" in any sin or habit which holds us captive. Anderson rightly observes:

> The diabolical idea that people are their own gods is the mantra of this fallen world and the primary link in the chain of spiritual bondage to the kingdom of darkness...If you desire to live in freedom from bondage of the world, the flesh and the devil, this primary link in the chain must be smashed.[2]

Your life is a time-sensitive trust from God. You get to choose how you will invest your life. Claim your identity as a child of God, your saved position in Christ, and live in his power to honor him daily. Pay attention to your spiritual life and keep your perspective on what is temporary and what is eternal. Choose to follow the guidance and teachings of those who lean heavily toward the eternal. Saturate your mind with the teachings of the sages who knew God and have passed on their wisdom through holy scriptures. Seek counsel from believers who are mature in their walk with God and stay connected with those who will encourage you in your walk of faith. Remain vigilant concerning what you take into your mind through TV, reading, or social media. Learn, through the wise counsel of scripture, how to distinguish what is good, bad, and neutral, and choose wisely.

Remember, Christ has saved you and will continue the work he has begun in you. Talk to him, confess your issues to him, and ask for his healing and deliverance, and he will provide all you need. You belong to Christ; remember that as you invest your time, money, and energies.

INVESTMENT REVIEW

1. Christianity teaches that you are accountable for how you invest your life. What does this truth imply about the need to understand yourself and the life maps you are following?

2. Identify some of the maps (ways of viewing life) that have shaped the way you invest your time, talents, energy and money.

3. Which of your maps need to be changed to more closely
    align with the teachings of Jesus?

4. What actions are you willing to take to change the way you
    think and act to live according to God's plan for your life?

CHAPTER FIVE

Your Awesome Power of Choice

*Behold, I set before you the way of life and the way
of death.*
—Jeremiah 21:8

Truth number four is "Your investment choices determine your character, which in turn determines your future." You might ask, "Are my choices an expression of my character or is my character formed by the choices I make?" I believe it is both; our choices reveal who we are as well as form our basic character. Let's explore how our choices and character are related.

Biblical Christianity teaches that choice and the corresponding responsibility for our choices are natural parts of being human. What is this "choice" capacity, and how does it relate to the value systems of the two worlds in which we live? Wise investors understand and use their power of choice responsibly.

How Choice Develops
What follows is a simplified overview of how choice develops and how the ability to decide affects our lives. Early in life, a child learns to distinguish between things that bring him pleasure or pain and

to make choices about what he does and does not like. At an early stage—some believe as early as four or five—he begins to develop a sense of right and wrong about his behavior. He is developing a conscience, the inborn capacity to use instincts and moral learning to choose between good and evil.

Much of his sense of right and wrong is heavily influenced by what his parents or caregivers teach him by word and example. While some value-laden information comes from school, church, TV, and many other sources, for most, the home is by far the dominant influence in moral development in the early years of most people.

How does a young child first come to think about God, the ultimate arbiter of right and wrong? While the young child does not understand God in abstract terms as an adult would, the practical reality is that his parents serve as the ultimate power and authority in his life, his first "god." Parents serve to provide the bridge to the God who made us and loves us. Trust is a critical issue in parenting and can establish or hinder a healthy relationship with God since that relationship is one of faith or trust also.

While the young child remains responsible to his parents for his choices, there comes the point in his moral development when he becomes directly accountable to God. Some have termed this the "age of accountability" and have established rituals such as baptisms or religious instruction classes or have identified the exact age at which this occurs for every child. I see this as a rather convenient but inadequate, and perhaps dangerous, attempt to deal with a more complex issue. Here are some questions about my concerns: Do all children have the same family situations from which they learn values? Do children within the same family have equal mental and spiritual capacities at the same age (e.g., age eight or twelve)? Is it possible for a child to become directly accountable to God at age ten, while a sibling may not become accountable until age fourteen or later?

One of the dangers I see in setting an arbitrary age when a person becomes directly accountable to God is that baptisms or other rituals that symbolize salvation can lead to a sense of false security. The issue is not age related but is more about whether the child realizes he is "lost" and can experience repentance and faith at a level where change takes place. If a person doesn't know he is a sinner and is "lost" from God, how can he be "saved"?

As the child matures into adolescence and youth, life becomes more complicated. A solid set of values becomes highly relevant because choices can have long-term consequences. As we progress through young adulthood and beyond, our value choices can be even more consequential and can set a pattern or direction which can bless or curse us. This ability to choose is awesome and, at times, a scary gift. You have an amazing ability to decide, to determine the kind of person you will become. You have the power to change your life by the decisions you make. Your choices will determine your character, and your character will determine your destiny.

We may not like the responsibility we have for making choices, but choices are a fundamental and vital part of life. And the choices we make can make all the difference to us. Choice is the power you have to determine the road you travel in life.

Why Your Choices Matter

To choose is to pick between two or more options, decide between alternatives, act in one way rather than another. To choose is to decide to favor one thing, option, or person over the other.

The ability to choose is God-given and involves both privilege and responsibility. While we have the freedom to make choices, we must realize our choices have consequences. Our choices can affect others as well as ourselves. Our decisions can result in good or bad effects in the near or distant future, and even in eternity. Why do I say these things?

The choices we make "make us." There is a real sense in which we become the product of our choices. Your choices have long-term, even eternal, meaning for you. Each of us has a value system of some sort, and those value choices shape our character, which in turn influences the significant decisions of our life.

Values precede decisions. Your value system can be a religious belief such as Christianity or some other faith. Some people do not ascribe to a religious belief system but have a code of honor or philosophy that informs their actions. We demonstrate our commitment to our professed values only to the degree that our actions are consistent with those beliefs. It is important to remember that every person has a value system, and that set of values is most evident in how we act, not in what we say we believe.

Your choices about values determine the kind of person you are. Your character, the single most important issue of life, is shaped by the choices you make about what is valuable to you. What are some of the value-reflecting decisions you make in the two-world culture in which you live?

Vocation is a choice and an expression of what we value in life. It matters how you earn a living because you are investing time and energy to do so. A great deal of satisfaction or frustration can result from this choice, and it is, therefore, essential to make a wise choice that is consistent with your deepest values.

Another highly important value-laden choice is whether or not to marry and whom to marry. It would be difficult to overstate the influence this choice has on the direction of one's life. There is no other human relationship fraught with as much potential for satisfaction or frustration as marriage. High degrees of maturity and understanding are required for a couple to have a good and functional relationship. Marriage is a serious commitment; a wrong decision here can lead to lots of pain and suffering. The choices we make do make us.

Choices tend to have a cumulative effect. What does that mean? The way you make choices now can become a pattern and carry over into your future. If you establish a pattern of making good choices, you will likely benefit by continuing to make good choices in your future. Bad or foolish decisions, if continued, will also have a cumulative effect on your future. This profound reminder of the power of our choices to affect your destiny should caution you to be sure you want to end up where your decisions are taking you: "Sow an act, and you reap a habit. Sow a habit, and you reap a character. Sow a character, and you reap a destiny."[1]

Once you have developed a habit of certain ways of making choices, that pattern is difficult to break. You can change a routine of making bad choices, but the longer the trend persists, the more challenging that becomes.

Since our choices determine our character and the kind of person we become, it is essential to get on the right path as early as possible. The habits of taking responsibility for your words and actions or blaming someone or something else, learning the value of work or being lazy, telling the truth, or lying to cover your mistakes—these choices will make your character. These decision-making patterns will persist in the two-world marketplace in which you live. If you are a parent, you will want to think about how important the early years are in helping your child learn how to make wise choices.

Wise people make good choices a habit. How can you get into the habit of making good choices? A habit is a way of acting that we develop and perfect through practice. Do you want to learn to play a game, develop good manners, maintain an exercise program, or stop doing something that is unhealthy or a waste of time and money? If so, pay close attention to these three things you will need to practice.

The first part of learning to consistently make good choices is doing the hard work of *acquiring knowledge about the issues or values involved in your decision.* Remember, sincere choices based on wrong information end up being bad decisions. While it may be challenging to know everything about a subject, be sure you have good information before taking a course of action. Seeking accurate information is particularly important in the four major decision areas mentioned earlier: character, faith, vocation, and marriage. The more consequential the decision, the more critical it is to have the right information or knowledge. Where can you get help?

Christian scriptures have served as a reliable source of wisdom for believers for centuries. Those who seek to understand and apply scriptural principles to problems or challenges will benefit from the experiences and wisdom of Abraham, Moses, Jacob, Jesus, Paul, and many others who have known and walked with God for many years.

Prayer and meditation can also lead to a sense of direction about a particular course of action. Allowing God to speak to you in quietness and prayer can be very helpful in determining what you are to do. It is essential to understand that God's leadership in this way will never contradict the clear teaching of scripture. And if scripture is already evident on an issue, there is no reason to pray for direction. In this case, our prayer should be for strength and help to obey what we already know to do.

Another important way to get the right information is to seek the counsel of a person who is wise and knowledgeable. I have been very fortunate to have had several older Christians to guide me through some difficult situations. The combination of scripture, prayer, and the wisdom of an experienced fellow believer can lead you to discover the will of God in your quest to know what to do.

The second part of making good choices has to do with *your willingness to act on your knowledge.* Once you have learned the right course of action, you must have a change of will, a commitment and determination to act on what is right. This commitment requires a willingness to face the fear and the consequences of the action you will take. This is a test of your character. Consistently making good choices requires us to make a habit of committing to trying to do what is right.

Making wise choices is much more complicated than making bad ones. It seems to be part of our nature to be lazy, rebellious, self-centered, and to make those choices that satisfy us quickly. We exercise our will to take the easy way, the road traveled by most.

Good choices are more difficult because they require a discipline of our will to take the long look, to put off immediate satisfaction, and to obey values based on truth, compassion, and fairness. To will, to choose, and to do what is consistent with what is right and good is to choose the narrow road less traveled.

Sometimes it is necessary to recognize that what is right to do is what we don't want to do, something that makes us uncomfortable. If this is the case, it is wise to acknowledge you are not at the place you should be to do what is needed. I have faced such times and admitted it to myself and God: "God, I know what I need to do, but I don't want to do it." To be obedient, I have asked God to help me come to the place where I am willing to do what I need to do. Patiently and lovingly, God has transformed my reluctance and unwillingness to willingness and obedience.

The third part of making a choice is to *follow through,* to act on the decision or course of action. If you have determined you should apologize to someone, take a risk on a business venture, or ask for a job interview, et cetera, you need to act. Good information and good intentions don't count for much without acting on them.

Sometimes God may lead you to simply wait or delay action on the issue at hand. As you pray and think about the situation, more information may come to light that will help you determine a wise course of action.

To summarize: Making a wise choice involves getting as much trustworthy information as you can about the subject, coming to a place where you are willing to act on what you have learned, and doing what you have come to believe is the right thing to do. If you understand and practice this process over time, wise decision making will become a habit, one that will reward you many times throughout your life.

For Your Consideration

The following tips may help you in using your God-given power to choose wisely:

Take responsibility for yourself. Own your feelings, thinking, and actions. Taking responsibility for yourself is a good sign you are maturing. Facing the consequences for your choices will demonstrate the wisdom of making good ones but can also help you learn to avoid bad ones.

Avoid making choices based on feelings alone. Feelings are often misinformed and can lead to bad decisions. Follow the guidance of scripture and the Spirit, or you may find yourself making many choices you may regret for a long time. Wait until you know your decision is based on faith that what you are doing is wise.

Consider the possible consequences of your choice. Avoid making big decisions or judgments on the spur of the moment. Stop, slow down, and think about the positive and negative consequences of your choice.

Talk to people wiser than yourself about your decision. Some decisions are so essential and life-altering that you need to seek the counsel and advice of a person you genuinely respect.

Write out your options—the pros and cons of your choice. You may find it very helpful to make pro and con columns at the top of a page and list the possible positives and negatives of a decision you are considering. There is something about getting it on paper that helps clarify the options and consequences of a choice.

Check your choice against good, solid values. Does this choice violate fundamental values such as honesty, fairness, compassion, generosity, and so on? Is the choice good for you in the long term? Is the decision consistent with your religious values?

You are given one life and the awesome power of choice to decide who you will be and what you will do with your life. You do have choices, and those choices have consequences. Who will you be? What will you value?

Life requires choices. The choice to follow Christ and learn how to navigate your way through your culture calls you to take the long look. Choosing the narrow road, the risky life of faith, is the only way to experience life at its best. You live in two worlds, and you must decide where you will invest your heart and resources.

Perhaps you are at a time when you need to decide to be serious about the profession of faith you have made. The most important decision you will ever make is to take the claim of Jesus personally and to follow him daily. You have the choice between two worlds, two roads. I pray you make the wise choice: "I shall be telling this with a sigh somewhere ages and ages hence: Two roads diverged in a wood, and I—I took the one less traveled by, and that has made all the difference." [2]

The choice is yours: the world and its treasures or Christ?

INVESTMENT REVIEW

1. What do your choices about the way you currently live say about your character?

2. What choices do you need to make that could have a profound effect on who you want to be?

3. Where do you expect to end up if you continue making the kinds of choices you are now making? Is this the destiny you want?

CHAPTER SIX

Time and Money

Why do you spend your money for what is not bread,
and your wages for what does not satisfy?
—Isaiah 55:2

Watching my parents struggle to make ends meet ingrained in me a sense of anxiety about having enough money for unexpected expenses. There were several situations we faced that created fear within me and fueled a determination to do everything I could to not be trapped in this seemingly endless cycle of uncertainty. The positive side of this has been that I have learned to live within my means. One of the most important things I have come to understand is that good investments bring good returns.

Money: End or Means?

As you may have gathered, I struggled with a delusion that money could solve an emotional need I had. I had become convinced it would calm my anxious spirit. When you confuse means with ends, your emotional life can get really out of balance. There is nothing in this world that can do for you what only God can do. The resources he provides are the means to an end, never ends in themselves.

I believe we have two major investment resources. One is money. The other is time. I have come to understand I have been wrong about the one I have long believed to be more important.

Let's talk about money. In my opinion, it is much less important than time. That idea may seem a bit preposterous because of the power and pleasure money can provide. Money is a deity to those who worship at the altar of power and materialism. From the world's vantage point, this does seem reasonable. Just think of what it can buy!

Money gives a person power and advantage in the world. It provides lots of desirable things: a car, a house, a vacation, and a second house on the beach. Money can buy votes and special favors. Sex, food, and drink and all kinds of pleasures can be had with it. You can buy life insurance, which is useful only if you die. And you can insure yourself from bankruptcy from catastrophic health issues with health insurance. But eventually, you will run out of time, die, and leave your money and possessions to someone else.

Money is important. In addition to all those things just mentioned, it is needed to provide food, clothing, housing, transportation, automobile and home insurance, and education for you and your family. You can use it to help those less fortunate and support the essential services of the government for yourself and others. You can give money to your church or religious organization to support their ministries. All these are good things.

Money or wealth is not evil. Like many things, it takes on moral or spiritual significance by the value a person attaches to it and how he uses it. While scriptural teachings do not condemn wealth, per se, there are strong warnings regarding its seductive power. For example, read what Paul writes to Timothy in 1 Timothy 6:9–10:

Those who want to get rich fall into temptation and a snare and many foolish and harmful desires which plunge men into ruin and destruction. For the love of money is a root of all sorts of evil, and some by longing for it have wandered away from the faith, and pierced themselves with many a pang.

Both the Old and New Testaments have lots to say about money and possessions. Here is a quick summary of my understanding of what the Bible teaches about money and possessions:

- God is the Creator and Owner of all the world's wealth and resources.

- We are created in God's image and are temporary stewards or managers of his resources. We ultimately own nothing.

- We are to manage and work with God's resources only in ways that honor him. We are to earn our livelihoods in a way that is consistent with God's laws. Those who are able are to work for their livelihoods and not depend on the charity of others.

- Possessions and riches can bring a false sense of security and obscure the need to put our trust in God. We must be careful not to trust in our riches, which we can quickly lose.

- We are to give generously to support ministries that promote the teaching of God's word and to meet the needs of others.

- We are to deal honestly and fairly with others in financial matters. We are to respect the rights of others to have possessions and not covet what they have or steal anything that belongs to them.

- We will die and leave all our money and possessions to someone else. We will take nothing with us but the character we have become.

- As managers, we are responsible to God for how we earn and use his resources. He will hold us accountable for how we manage what he has placed at our disposal.

Money and Character

Do you have any idea about the amount of money you may earn in your lifetime? Let's assume you are thirty years old and working your way up the organizational ladder. Or maybe you are an entrepreneur, trying to make it in a venture in something you really enjoy doing. Suppose you will be working until age sixty-five, thirty-five years, at a low ball earnings average of $55,000 per year over your working years. Of course, inflation and taxes will take a big bite out of your earnings, but your gross income based on these assumptions will be $1,925,000!

Just for the fun of it, let's look at some more numbers. During that same thirty-five years, an average income of $70,000 will amount to $2,450,000!

If you are a professional person, it is likely that your earnings over a lifetime will double, triple, or quadruple the $1.9 million of the person who averages $55,000 a year! Kind of mind boggling, isn't it, that you could make and be accountable for using all that money? Whether you are rich, poor, or in between, you will have at your disposal financial assets that will, in turn, be used to purchase and invest in things you value. Some of the items you buy will be used up or eventually end up in a landfill. You will also have the option to use your money to support purposes that will outlast you and follow you into your eternal home.

Money is a neutral asset, not good or bad in and of itself. It is yours to use. You can make it a security god or purchase your pleasure god with it. You can squander it or hoard it or use it to provide for your needs and to help others. It's your choice, and the choices you make about its use say a great deal about who you are as a person, your character, and what is important to you.

If you believe your character is important, then you cannot escape the necessity of reckoning with what your use of money and possessions says about you. The way you earn and use money and possessions is one of the most accurate measures of what you value. Remember, you demonstrate your real character by how you act. So how you behave with money and possessions is a pretty accurate measure about which of the two worlds has a stronger hold on you.

Time and Character

Time is the other major resource at your disposal. One reason for contending that it is more important than money is because it is not replaceable. I know of several people who have gone bankrupt but have, with wise decisions and effort, replaced homes, bank accounts, automobiles, and most other possessions. It is a fact that money and things can be replaced. No one has been able to regain time that has passed; when it's gone, it's gone for good.

What happens when you spend your time? No matter how you choose to use it, *you can't get it back*. Can you magically roll back the calendar and relive a day or time you used poorly? Of course not. Can you go back to when your children were young and spend more time nurturing and encouraging them in their development as competent, responsible people? No, that time and those opportunities are gone forever.

The kind of time I'm thinking about as your primary investment resource is that span of life that occurs between the beginning of life and your death, your fifty, sixty, or seventy years to live. It's that dash on your tombstone representing your time in this world. It could be much shorter than the normal life span, or you could be among the relatively few centenarians. You don't know how long you will live, but you do know this: your life is a time-sensitive trust.

Time is important, and the marketplace knows it. The marketplace has certainly paid attention to the ways you use your minutes, hours, and days. Many products are designed to help you "save" time. Microwave ovens, fast-food restaurants, and meals ready to pop in the oven and on the table in ten minutes are part of the market's emphasis on saving you time. Fast cars, trains, and planes save you time by moving you from one place to another quickly. There are convenience markets, express lines, and almost every imaginable gadget or service to use less of the one thing you will eventually use up.

Ironically, it seems many people are more frazzled and distracted than ever before because they keep filling their "saved" time with more things that are supposed to save them even more time. The marketplace is telling you time is important, but it tends to sell us things that do not satisfy our deepest needs.

Maybe you've just never thought of how valuable your time really is. Time is unlike money in that it is limited, and you don't get it back once it is gone. Also, time is not tangible, something you can handle, like money or physical possessions. But it is like money in the sense that you can trade or exchange it for something you want, need, or consider necessary.

You exchange time for money, giving many hours each week for the compensation you will, in turn, exchange for food, housing, and many other things. You use time when you sleep, take a shower, and prepare for visitors or an important meeting. You spend time reading or watching TV. You invest time talking with your children, spouse, or friends. Every day you trade twenty-four hours of your life for work, sleep, eating, and doing many other things. Some of your time investments are for necessities, while others are discretionary. However you decide to use your time, one thing is true: once you spend it, you don't get it back.

In our younger days, my two brothers and I got together for some fun times on the golf course near our home. The one agreement we made before teeing off was about how many mulligans we could take during the eighteen holes. The dictionary defines a *mulligan* as an Irish stew. I can only guess why the term became associated with golf. Perhaps it meant if you were in trouble or "in the stew," you could have another try to undo the bad shot you had made. My brothers and I generally agreed to two mulligans, or redos, for lousy tee shots.

But that was a game where we could make rules to accommodate our lack of skill. Life is not so generous; we don't get to change the rules. That means we don't get a mulligan to undo time wasted or misspent—no second chances to use those minutes, hours, days, months, and years over.

Another complicating fact about time is that there is no guarantee of how much of it we really have, how many years we have to live. A quick scan of a recent obituary will prove my point; people of all age groups die daily. One thing we can be sure of is that our name will appear in the obit someday. There is only one exception to the certainty of our death: the scriptural teaching that believers who are alive at the return of Christ to earth will not face death.

One of the few things I remember most about the Latin classes I took in high school is the term *Tempus fugit*, which means "Time flies." On the face of a clock hanging in the foyer of my home is the picture of a clock with wings. Under the picture are those Latin words, *Tempus fugit*. Our time on earth has wings and is quickly flying away.

Statistics show that approximately 7,400 people run out of time every day in the United States, 156,000 worldwide. Men average 76.3 years in length of life, while women are living to an average of 81 years. What do these statistics tell you about how many minutes, hours, days, months, and years you will live? Nothing! They indicate the average life span of a collective group of people. While your death is guaranteed, you cannot be sure when you will have used up your last second of time. Today could be your last. Who knows?

Some people tend to ignore the reality that their life has a time limit on it. They use their time unwisely, without a sense of purpose, and squander opportunities to better themselves and make positive contributions to their families and the broader community. Some of these same folks will look back on those years with regret, wishing they could have those hours and days again. They would like to have a do-over, but no amount of money or wishing will change the fact that those times and opportunities are gone. They are gone forever.

Others live as if they are scared of death and rush about trying to cram in every pleasure they can before their time runs out. Their anxiety and appetites control their lives. They live as if this world is all there is, and they indulge every taste and desire they have.

Our life is a gift from God, and we are to use our time in ways that honor him. So how are we to invest our time wisely? Think about how you will answer this question in light of what Paul instructs us to do in Ephesians 5:15–16: "Therefore, be careful how you walk, not as unwise men but as wise, making the most of your time, because the days are evil."

While you cannot undo bad choices you may have made in the past, you can learn from your mistakes and choose to invest more wisely beginning today. In the later chapters of this book, you will be challenged to consider some specific ways you can invest your remaining time in the things that matter most and maximize the return of your life's investments.

INVESTMENT REVIEW

1. What does the way you use money say about your character?

2. What does the way you use time say about your character?

3. What are some things you can add or eliminate that would lead to better use of your time?

4. What would you change about the way you use your time and money if you knew you only had one year to live?

CHAPTER SEVEN

Change Your Thinking; Change Your Life

As he thinks within himself, so he is.
—Proverbs 23:7

I am a planner; I have been for many years. Writing out goals and strategies gets ideas out of my head and into a visible form. This process helps me refine, organize, and prioritize goals and decide how to invest my time and resources. Having a written plan also serves to hold me accountable for getting things done.

There's an old saying that goes like this: "He who fails to plan plans to fail." Those who make daily to-do lists and those who plan ten or twenty years down the road have something significant in common. They have a goal, something to be accomplished, whether it is to meet someone for lunch or have a million dollars in assets in ten years. Our plans are expressions of what is important to us and what we want to do about those things.

The Power of Your Thinking

The way we think about life determines the ways in which we plan or do not plan to live. In chapter three, I told you how my feelings and actions were influenced by the way I interpreted some of my childhood experiences. One of the great lessons I've learned is this: how I interpret an experience reflects my view of reality and tends to influence my behavior. My sense of reality can be different from the truth, which only God knows completely. Think about that. Your view of reality, your interpretation of what's happening, is based on the limited facts you have and how you tend to process those partial pieces of information. For example, if you are an untrusting person, you will likely come to unwarranted conclusions about a situation and act in unjustified ways. If you are honest and caring, you change your mind when information comes to light that proves your initial thinking to be wrong.

God has given us the ability to choose. I can choose to live the lies I have believed or replace them with his truth. My maps, how I have learned to think about life, influence all my plans and how I want to invest. Being aware of my maps' power to influence my decisions allows me to think about and decide to make different choices. With God's help, I can choose to break their emotional hold and begin making choices that align with the gospel. The biblical idea of repentance is to change our minds, turn around, or choose a different way of acting. Repentance toward God means I choose to accept and live according to what he says is right. I agree with God; I choose to think as he thinks and act according to his standards.

In the process of forming my maps, I made some promises to myself. One pledge that had a strong impact had to do with money. This was an unconscious or emotional determination to earn enough not to be embarrassed in situations such as I faced in childhood. As a young kid, I mowed yards, picked strawberries at local farms, and ordered and sold greeting cards in my neighborhood. At one point,

I ventured into the livestock business. On two or three occasions, Dad took me to the local stock sale, where I bought a young calf so I could fatten it for resale at the same market. I bought a feeder bucket and the formula mix necessary to put lots of pounds on the young animal. After several months of feeding and taking care of the calf, we took the much larger animal back to the market, where I got a good return on my investment.

Outwardly, my actions appeared smart and industrious, but my motive was faulty. I was scared of being embarrassed or not having enough. My goal was simple. I wanted to have spending money of my own and not depend on my parents to buy things I wanted or needed for myself. This anxiety persisted through my college and graduate school experiences. Looking back, I think I was in a financial survival mode. After marriage and children, the picture of life got bigger, and I had to consider how to adequately provide for my family. The pressure increased.

There was an emotional split in my life. I trusted God for my salvation but emotionally lived like I was on my own. But through all this, God was patiently teaching me that he has a master plan for my life and that I could trust him to provide for my needs. Gradually, my thinking became more aligned with scriptural truth, and healing took place. Consequently, there has been a reordering of priorities in my life, a sense of wholeness and integration.

Big-Picture Thinking

This growing awareness of God's love for me and my surrender in repentance and faith put me on a life journey that has progressively brought about a significant shift in my thinking and actions related to money and possessions. I have come to see my time and possessions as gifts, a means to an end. This big-picture idea of life has challenged and inspired me to focus all my resources on the purpose for which God has created me.

The process I am describing has taken several years and resulted in a life goal around which I have attempted to organize my life. Before developing this life statement, I had some general idea of God's plan for my life. However, the disciplined thinking process and prayers about my gifts and passion for life brought me to another level of commitment. There was one more step I needed to take. That step was to develop a written expression of the values that would give direction to my daily living. After a few attempts, I came up with a statement that resonates with my core beliefs and provides a focus for my life.

My experience as a Christian has involved several growth periods, times when my understanding and commitment deepened. Most of these "paradigm shifts" have been gradual, as my thinking evolved to a clearer grasp of what it means to follow Jesus. For example, along the way of learning the basics of living as a Christian, I realized that God has a dual claim on my life. He has created me, and he has saved me. The overriding implication of this truth is that I belong to him, and my highest calling is to know him and serve him through what he has given me. The step of putting these ideas into a life statement has crystallized my shift in thinking and provides a great tool to keep me focused on the things that matter most to me.

Here is the simple declaration that has guided me for many years: "My purpose in life is to honor Christ and my family through my personal and professional relationships." That goal or purpose statement defines what I'm about and provides a foundation on which I seek to build the superstructure of my life. This philosophical declaration is my statement of religion, the way I want to live my life. It also provides a framework to plan and express my faith in daily living.

Here are some implications of how my purpose statement translates into everyday living. First, Christ is supreme in my life.

I belong to him, and it is my purpose, my joy, to honor him in all I do. My family is the next priority. I will do all within my power to respect my marriage and take my parenting responsibilities seriously. And I will take the same sense of respect for Christ and my family to work and all relationships with friends, associates, and people I encounter in the everyday flow of life.

I have spent countless hours thinking, reading, and praying about the practical implications of what it means to put my life goal into practice. These actions have led me to consider things I could do to get to know Christ better and encourage family members and others. My weekly to-do list includes devotional time, exercise, reading, a contact to check on someone, or something I can do to honor my wife and children and others in my circle of influence. Keeping my goal in front of me helps me stay focused on the things that matter most and challenges me to make wise investments of my time, money, and energies.

A Challenge for You

Do you have a life goal, an overriding purpose that is worthy of the time, energy, and financial resources God has placed in your care? If not, why not consider it? If you had a million dollars to invest, would you do some serious thinking about what you wanted to do with it? Or would you drift along without a goal or appreciation of what you could accomplish with that small fortune?

God has placed great value on the life he has given you. Your life is a time-sensitive trust, worth far more than any amount of money or possessions you can ever accumulate. The accurate measure of God's valuation of you is the price he paid for you when he allowed Christ to die for you at Calvary. Surely you wouldn't be so foolish to squander a fortune, would you?

You have a great treasure to invest in the marketplace of the two-world system in which you live. Both worlds put a claim on you.

I encourage you to set your goals on things that will last long after you have spent your time and have taken your last breath: "He is no fool who gives up what he cannot keep for what he cannot lose." [1]

INVESTMENT REVIEW

1. What are some shifts in thinking and acting that have brought your life into a closer alignment with God's plan for your life?

2. Is there an area of your life where God is challenging you to change your thinking and acting so that he can bless you further?

3. How do you think a purpose statement could help you focus on those things that are most important in your life?

CHAPTER EIGHT

Getting on the Right Path

*Enter by the narrow gate; for the gate is wide, and the
way is broad that leads to destruction, and many are
those who enter by it. For the gate is small, and the way
is narrow that leads to life, and few are those who
find it.*
—Matthew 7:13–14

I assume that you, like most people, want to have a sense of purpose in your life. You want to know that you have mattered to someone or to something of worth in your lifetime. However, I believe that sense of meaning is missing in lots of folks who hurry through life without ever coming to understand the why of their existence.

I believe we have the choice between a right path and a wrong path in life. There is only one way to live that is consistent with reality. Love is the ultimate reality, and those who choose to invest their heavenly currency in the things that matter most are on the right path.

Heaven's Currency is concerned with how you invest your life. I want you to understand that there is much more to life than money and wealth; my concern is that you focus on God's plan for your life. Your character influences every important decision of your life. Therefore, let's take a brief look at some things people of excellent character do in their approach to investing.

Timely Wisdom from an Old Story

Let's get started by gleaning some wisdom from one of Aesop's stories, "The Goose That Laid the Golden Egg." As you may remember, the farmer discovers he has an unusual goose (resource); it lays golden eggs! After he and his wife collect these treasures for some time, they realize this goose can quickly change the whole trajectory of their lives. The goose is their key to instant wealth. They are convinced they can immediately have all the marvelous things they have ever wanted. The goose is their ticket! In their state of excitement and lack of forethought, greed takes over, and they kill the goose and extract all the golden eggs at once. Of course, you know what this means.

This fable, centuries-old, speaks of the human propensity to exchange long-term gain for immediate satisfaction, to "kill the goose" to satisfy our lust for treasures in the here and now. Like the farmer and his wife, we often fail to take the long look and foolishly squander our resources on things that are not of lasting worth. For this reason, it is wise to consider ideas that can help you make the right decisions about the path you want to travel in life.

As I have already stated, I firmly believe we have choices to make about resources other than money or possessions. These gifts are more valuable and meaningful than any amount of money or things we could accumulate. Furthermore, I think most of us would do well to treat these resources with the kind of seriousness wise investors have toward their financial investments. God has given each of us a "goose" that has great potential for good: our life and all we need to live within his plan. Don't foolishly squander the gift God has given you. Please consider how the following ideas can put you on the right path to wisely invest your life and resources in those things with eternal value.

Embrace God's plan. To build an adequate plan for life, you must first understand and commit to the big picture, the purpose or idea that God has for you.

First, you must accept the fact of who God is and who you are. You are a created being, and God, your Creator, has a purpose for you. God loves you and wants the best for you. He has provided everything you need to live within his plan, but you must choose to do so. Furthermore, God holds you accountable for the life and possessions he has entrusted to you.

Now here's the rub. Like Adam in Eden, you and I must confront the universal challenge of all humankind. Who or what will be God? Do you trust the word of God and live in obedience to him? Do you give ultimate allegiance to something other than God? Do you assume the role of God for yourself and live in rebellion? God's big-picture idea of life is that you commit to a relationship with him, where there is no rival to his lordship. He will be your God, or he will not be your God at all. Recall Jesus's explicit statement about this matter: "No one can serve two masters...you cannot serve God and mammon" (Matt. 6:24).

If you want to be serious about following Jesus, you must surrender your will to live according to God's plan. The plan calls for you to put him first, love him above all else, and love others as you love yourself. To do this requires nothing less than a spiritual conversion in which you allow God's Spirit to begin and continue the process of developing the character of Jesus in you.

The bottom line is this: God created you and wants to make you into a new creation. And he will do that if you put your faith in him. To follow him means to confess him as your Savior and agree with him about what is right for you to do. Your life in Christ begins with a repentance that brings forgiveness of your sin. To grow to be like Jesus requires humility, which allows you to change the way you think and act as the Spirit prompts you.

At the close of the Sermon on the Mount in Matthew 7:21 and 24–27, Jesus tells us that our real success or failure in life depends on the critical choice we make to live within God's plan:

> Not everyone who says to me, "Lord, Lord," will enter the kingdom of heaven; but he who does the will of my father who is in heaven…Therefore, everyone who hears these words of mine and acts on them may be compared to a wise man who built his house on the rock. And the rain descended, and the floods came, and the winds blew and burst against that house, and yet it did not fall for it had been founded upon a rock. And everyone who hears these words of mine and does not act upon them will be like a foolish man who built his house upon the sand. And the rain descended, and the floods came, and the winds blew and burst against the house, and it fell, and great was its fall.

Wise investors embrace God's plan.

Set specific goals concerning God's plan. OK. So you get it. God wants all of you. He demands that you live honorably in this present culture in the various roles and responsibilities you have. But how do you live out the plan God has for you?

Your clue about specific goals is in the statement Jesus made in Matthew 22:37–39. Look carefully: "You shall love the Lord your God with all your heart, and with all your soul, and with all your mind. This is the great and foremost commandment. And a second is like it; you shall love your neighbor as yourself."

What exactly are you committing to do when you embrace God's plan? Have you worked on a box puzzle? If so, you likely used the picture on the box to reference what all the pieces should represent when you finished. Likewise, it's wise to understand God's view of the meaning and purpose of life as you make specific goals and plans for your life.

Let's follow the box puzzle analogy a bit further. The picture "on the box" represents the scripture just referenced. And what does the scripture picture tell us? Our life is about the three relationships: God, self, and others. This is the big picture. We find true meaning and purpose in life as we live in a loving relationship with God, ourselves, and others.

From this understanding of God's purpose, you might develop your life purpose statement to say something like this, "To put God and his purpose first in my life and to love others as I love myself." Take some time to think deeply about your big-picture plan because it will be the foundation on which you will develop specific goals and steps to give direction to your life.

If you have been convinced of the wisdom to embrace God's plan and have committed to giving yourself 100 percent, it is time to do some serious planning. Once you have your statement in place, you are ready to develop specific plans to make it happen.

One way to approach this plan for your life is to identify separate pieces of your goal and develop strategies related to those areas. For example, you can make one part of your goal "Put God first in my life." Then you will ask the question: How do I plan to put God first in my life? Your plans or actions may include actions such as the following:

- To learn about God and his will through the study of and meditation on scripture each day.

- To seek to understand specific ways in which the scriptures apply to my life.

- To obey what I am learning from scripture in all my relationships.

This focus on scripture is an excellent way to accomplish your plan to put God first in every aspect of your life. Praying, worshipping, reading, and seeking the wisdom of mature believers could be other areas in which to develop plans to accomplish your goal. More detailed examples of this process are found in Parts Two and Three of this book.

You will not drift into godliness. You must be proactive and deliberate for God's plan to be accomplished in your life. God will do the spiritual change and growth in you, but you must cooperate by putting plans in place that allow this to happen. Make definite plans about using your week to honor God, and break this down into daily bites to accomplish your weekly goal. Don't attempt to accomplish everything in one day or one week. Be patient, plan wisely, and hold yourself accountable to achieve your goals.

What you are embarking upon is a day-by-day challenge that will require persistence. Proverbs 6:6 speaks of the wisdom and work mentality of the ant, one of God's smallest creatures, as an example for us to emulate: "Go to the ant, O sluggard, observe her ways and be wise."

Be diligent and persistent like the ant. Don't give up. Plan to make progress each day and act upon your ideas, and little by little, you will realize how God is working to shape you into the person he has created you to be. Take heart. Stay the course, and watch God work: "Soon, the accomplishments of each day are gathered, one atop another, like the ant piles his grains of sand, and eventually a castle is erected large enough to house any dream."[1]

Be proactive. Write out your goals in specific, measurable terms. Plan how you will use your time, money, and energies to love God above all else and to love others as you love yourself. Have a plan for each day.

Prioritize your goals. To accomplish important goals, you must be realistic and strategic in planning and using your available resources. To live within God's plan, you must distinguish between wants and needs and choose their relative importance. What do you need to do to develop a godlier character? Are there useless wants or habits such as excessive TV, overeating junk food, or time wasters that do not contribute to your well-being?

Don't be alarmed; prioritizing your goals will not take all the fun or enjoyment out of life. Putting first things first will create a balance that will help you invest your time, money, and energy in those areas that matter most. Living healthily in our hectic, fast-paced world requires a sense of equilibrium that seems to be missing in so many. Prioritize and simplify.

Expect there to be times you will need to give up something good for something better. For example, you and your family may have made a strong effort to be out of debt within a specified amount of time. You have drastically cut back on eating out, cut out cable, and are working hard to pay off all debt except for your house. Making choices such as these just mentioned is an excellent example of what it means to prioritize. You give up something you may want to achieve what is best.

When you prioritize your goals, changes will come in the ways you spend time, money, and energy. You will recognize the necessity of a new way of doing things for a couple of reasons. First, you have limited resources. It is unrealistic to live as if you have unlimited energy, time, and money. Most people must control their spending to purchase priorities such as housing, food, clothing, education, and insurance. Likewise, your time is limited. Rest, work, family life, and other commitments require time. When you overcommit your time or money, something has to suffer. Prioritizing your goals will help you allot your limited resources to your highest priorities. Never exchange the "best" for the "good."

Prioritizing can also help you make some tough choices when goals come into conflict. It is easy to see how this could happen with the busy lifestyles we have. For example, your family has decided to have one meal together on Sunday, Tuesday, and Thursday. You have committed to making this a tradition to promote unity and communication in your family. This goal means that family members make no commitments to dates that conflict with this family priority. While prioritizing your goals can be a complicated process, it has a definite upside of helping you make decisions about things that do not support your priorities.

Evaluate your results and adjust as needed. Building your character is much like building a house. Both have a foundation on which everything else depends. Upon that foundation, you will create the superstructure and all the details of your life. And, as in the process of constructing a house, you need to evaluate progress and adjust to get the result you want.

Let's follow this analogy a little further. You've chosen your house plan, and the work is underway when your contractor runs into a snag. He explains the additional costs involved and the options to keep the project within budget. You attempt to understand why things haven't gone according to plans and decide to correct the situation.

The same is true in building a godly, Christ-like character. You may have failed to use your anger wisely and lost your cool with a family member or work associate and need to address what you said or did that was wrong. Evaluate and adjust. Hold yourself accountable, and take appropriate actions to fix the issue. Ask God to forgive you, help you learn from your sin, and ask the person you have offended to forgive you.

Acknowledge when you have failed. Repent and move on. There will be days when you can meet your goals. Celebrate, give God credit, and keep going. Remember, you are in a marathon, not a hundred-yard sprint.

Being a true disciple is no wimpy matter. It involves much more than being saved to ensure we don't burn forever in the fires of hell. Following Jesus requires a commitment to give all we are to obey him and become like him. To paraphrase the words of C. S. Lewis, "God doesn't want to trim a limb here and there; he wants the whole tree down." Paul makes a stunning statement about God's plan for us in Romans 8:29. God has determined that we "become conformed to the image of His Son." We are to take on the personality and actions of Jesus in the marketplace where he has placed us.

To do this, we must first accept God's goal and continually learn more about Jesus and how we need to adjust our life to be more like him. Evaluate and adapt.

Stay with it. There will be discouraging times as you try to follow the Lord. People may disappoint you, but God is faithful and will supply the courage you need to endure. Your growth is a process that will take time and patience. Remember, the ultimate goal God has for your life is to make you like Christ. You have taken a giant step when you agree with God and commit to cooperating with his plan. So stay with it.

Consider the resources God has made available for you to accomplish His plan. Hebrews says long ago, "God, after he spoke long ago to the fathers in the prophets in many portions and in many ways, in these last days has spoken to us in His Son...the exact representation of His nature" (Heb. 1:1–3). Today, you have scriptures that tell you about Jesus, and you have the Spirit of Jesus, who lives within you to teach and guide you in understanding scripture and what God wants for you. The Spirit of Jesus will always agree with the will of God, as expressed in scripture.

The changes you experience in the way you think and act will move you closer to who God created you to be. You will discover that while you can get further along, there will be no end to your spiritual growth in this life. Paul, perhaps Jesus's most ardent follower, said:

> I count all things to be loss in view of the surpassing value of knowing Jesus Christ my Lord, for whom I have suffered the loss of all things, and count them as rubbish that I may gain Christ. And may be found in Him, not having a righteousness of my own derived from the Law, but the righteousness that comes from God on the basis of faith... Not that I have already obtained it, or have already become perfect, but I press on in order that I may lay hold of that for which also I was laid hold of by Christ Jesus (Phil. 3:8–9, 12).

INVESTMENT REVIEW

1. How does Aesop's fable in this chapter apply to your life and society in general?

2. Where are you concerning the four steps for developing your character?

3. What specific areas or issues has God been prompting you to resolve?

4. What do you need to do to grow to be more like Jesus?

5. Why are endurance and adjustment so critical in developing a Christlike character?

PART TWO

Investing to Maximize Your ROI

CHAPTER NINE

Building Your Portfolio

You shall love the Lord your God with all your heart,
and with all your soul, and with all your mind...You
shall love your neighbor as yourself.
—Matthew 22:37, 39

Each of us has an investment portfolio of some type. Carelessness regarding how we build it will bring loss and disappointment when we most need the return on our investment. Just as there are two world marketplaces that beckon to us, there are two portfolios we are putting together: one with temporary investments that can be lost and another that promises an eternal ROI. First, let's look at the one we are probably more familiar with: our temporal portfolio.

What's in Your Portfolio?

The word *portfolio* is sometimes used to refer to a briefcase or some other kind of instrument to carry important papers or documents. But we generally use the term to refer to the types of securities or investments we have purchased. If a financial adviser asks, "What's in your portfolio?" they are asking about the kinds and amounts of investments you have bought.

Your portfolio may be focused entirely on offerings on the stock market. However, within the stock market, your investments may be diversified in stocks and bonds. For example, you may have assets distributed among some bonds as well as large, medium, and small companies. Further, you may have investments that spread among US companies as well as the international market. Your portfolio may reveal you have an interest in a myriad of sectors, such as health care, transportation, high tech, and entertainment. The options seem endless, and the diversification is intended to balance your investments to protect against loss and give you an excellent long-term ROI.

You may forgo the market entirely and diversify your portfolio with land, rental property, precious metals, antiques, a house-flipping endeavor, personal business, vintage automobiles, or a second home. Your primary concern is to get the biggest bang for your buck without losing your principal investment. While some immediate appreciation can take place, you may build your portfolio with the expectation of medium- to long-term gains and pay attention to the best time to buy and sell in that particular market.

What Motivates Your Investing?

According to the 2020 census, over ten million Americans are millionaires, and more than a thousand are billionaires. What motivates people to build such enormous financial portfolios? Is it power, security, competition, the thrill of the challenge, generosity, legacy, or greed? Who knows? The answer is probably as varied as the individuals themselves and the types of investments that have made them rich. It is heartening to see many of these wealthy people building companies that offer jobs to many.

It is also encouraging to learn how generous some of these rich people are in the distribution of their wealth to help others.

Recently, I was drawn to a TV interview with one of the billionaires in our country. His name I did recognize, but his story told me he understood he was not only building a financial portfolio but a spiritual one as well. He is now in his eighties, and his life goal is to give all he has to help others. For many years he has built successful businesses and donated billions of dollars to hospitals and other needed work. In the interview, he expressed great joy in being able to invest his earnings to meet people's needs. At the close of the interview, he said something to the effect of, "God has put me here to help people. I plan to die broke."

If you have had the good fortune to work with a competent financial adviser, they have spent time helping you consider your goals and the kinds of investments that will meet your needs. They may have recommended specific sectors of stocks and diverse opportunities in addition to the stock market. You have taken your adviser's recommendations and built your portfolio because you trust your adviser's fiduciary commitment to look out for your best interests.

The Invested Life

One of the foundational assumptions I have made in this book is that our life is an investment. The choices we make with time, money, and energy are the contents of our life portfolio. In many ways, this portfolio is similar to our financial one.

Since this way of thinking could be a bit new to you, let's take a moment to see how it may be similar to and different from your financial portfolio. Your monetary wealth in your financial portfolio is the total of all your financial investments and possessions minus any debt or outstanding obligations. Your life portfolio is much broader in scope than your financial one. It includes how you have invested your money as well as your time and energy. If your main goal is to create wealth, then that is your life's primary purpose. Wealth is the end to be gained.

If you endorse the spiritual view that life has the higher purpose of serving God and others, you see money, time, energies, and possessions as means to that end. There is a stark contrast in these portfolios because the very reason for their existence is different. One is selfish, and the other focuses on service.

Both the financial and life portfolios belong to you, a mortal human being whose control of those investments will end at your death. However, as seen in the example of the billionaire, the investments you make in your life can have tremendous temporal benefits as well as eternal significance. When viewed in this light, your choices concerning how you earn "your" money and use it and your time and talents become something worth serious consideration.

Smart investors understand their principal and ROI are only as sound as the foundation or quality of the equities they are purchasing. There needs to be a good track record or something about the opportunity itself that indicates the likelihood of success. The foundation has to be trustworthy, or it will crumble in the ups and downs of the economy.

The same is true in life. If you do not invest in a reliable, dependable spiritual foundation, you will lose the very meaning and purpose of the life for which God has created you. I believe the billionaire referenced earlier has learned to make wise decisions about the financial and spiritual foundations on which he would build his fortunes. It's wonderful to see people do it right in both worlds!

I ask again, "What is your life goal or purpose?" Your answer will indicate the kinds of investments that are the foundation of your life portfolio. Your time, money, and energy will follow your heart.

If life is a resource for investing, what are the best investments you can make?

Investing and Life's Purpose

So what is the "end" or goal of life? If you can know this, you can choose to build your life portfolio on those things that will produce good results in this life as well as eternity. While there are many scriptural teachings on the subject of life's purpose, the one I think most clearly spells it out is in Matthew 22:36–40. I touched on this in an earlier chapter but want to go into more detail here to reinforce the importance of this scriptural concept.

In this passage, an expert in the Mosaic Law asks Jesus, "Teacher, which is the great commandment in the Law?" The lawyer is asking essentially the same question we are trying to answer: What is the highest goal or purpose of life? And Jesus's response shows us what we have been looking for, an essential clue to life's ultimate meaning.

How does he answer? He is explicit and direct: "You shall love the Lord your God with all your heart, and with all your soul, and with all your mind." And he adds the corollary: "And, a second is like it, 'You shall love your neighbor as yourself.' On these two commandments depend the whole Law and the Prophets."

There you have it. If you want to build your portfolio on what Jesus has said is most important, you will choose to learn how to love God, yourself, and others. There are two critical ideas to be extracted from Jesus's summation of the law and the prophets that guide us concerning the foundational investment of our life.

First, life's highest meaning and purpose are in our relationships. Both Old and New Testaments teach this through the law, the prophets, and most clearly in the teachings of our Lord and those whose gospels and letters we have to study.

There are warnings throughout scripture to never substitute anything for God's rightful place and to always act justly and kindly to others. The Ten Commandments are a prime example of how we are to show love or respect for him and others. Integrity, faithfulness, compassion, forgiveness, and generosity are to characterize the vertical and horizontal relationships of God's people. Relationships are the most crucial consideration when deciding how to build our life.

Second, Jesus uses the word *love* to describe the nature of our relationships with God and others. The apostle John says in 1 John 4:8, "The one who does not love does not know God, for God is love." The essence of God's character is love. This love is behind all he does. But notice what else is here. The person who does not love does not know God. The flip side of this statement means that the person whose life is characterized by love knows God intimately, personally. Love is heaven's currency.

Our culture's view of love is remarkably shallow when compared to the biblical understanding of what is meant by God's love and the love that is to characterize the followers of Jesus. The Greek word for *love* in John 3:16 ("God so loved the world") is the same as that in John 13:35, where Jesus says his disciples' identity with him is their love for each other. Likewise, it is the identical word used by our Lord when he tells us to love our enemies. It is the Greek word *agape* (αγαπε), the same as that just cited in 1 John 4:8.

The term *agape*, rarely used outside the early Christian community, takes on a unique meaning as the New Testament writers describe the Father's care for his children. Jesus uses this word in his teachings concerning our treatment of both friends and enemies. Paul employs the same term in 1 Corinthians 13 to identify the greatest of all spiritual qualities we are to pursue. Our Father shows his love by providing and doing for us what is in our best interest, not what we think is our best interest. His greatest concern is that we grow to be more and more like Jesus, and he will work in every circumstance to help that happen. God shows us what heaven's currency is by what it (his love) does for us.

In turn, we love others by doing what is best for them. We love our spouses, children, parents, neighbors, enemies, and business associates when we seek to do what is best for them. Only the transforming love of God in us can enable us to do this. Heaven's currency is provided in abundance to us once we decide to love God above all else.

The bottom line about the meaning of life is this: we are to live in loving obedience to God, our Father, grow into a genuinely caring person like Jesus, and treat others in ways that honor them and seek the best for them.

INVESTMENT REVIEW

1. Your life is your greatest investment opportunity. Since this is true, how would you evaluate the way you are using heaven's currency with your time, money, and energy?

2. What do your investments indicate about the kind of person you are?

3. In what ways do you think our culture distorts the idea of what it means to love another person?

4. What is the proof you are a follower of Jesus?

CHAPTER TEN

Loving God

*You shall love the Lord your God with all your heart,
and with all your soul, and with all your mind.*
—Matthew 22:37

Now, let's consider some implications of what it means to love God, to make him the centerpiece or foundation of your life. If you are a Christian, putting God first is your calling. Your faith commitment to him is the foundation on which you will build your life portfolio.

Knowing God Personally

When we talk about loving God, it is imperative to understand the difference between knowing about God and knowing God personally. There are theological seminaries and divinity schools throughout this country and the world where you can learn "about" God. You may receive a degree from one of these institutions, but that doesn't guarantee you will know God. You may learn to love ideas about God but not love him in a personal way, in a relationship like you have with people you care about.

God loves you and wants you to know and love him on a deep, personal level. Knowing about God is important because that can lead you to the point where you know him personally. For example, through your senses you realize you and the world around you came from somewhere, a Creator. Through experience you learn you have a moral nature and often fail to do your best, and experience a sense of guilt. In time, this knowing about God gets more personal. Somehow, through parents, friends, or a Bible teacher you learn that this Creator loves you and has a plan for your life. You also learn that to live in his plan requires you to put your trust in him, to accept the death, burial, and resurrection of Jesus for the forgiveness of your sin.

By an act of faith, you accept God at his word and begin a life of faith in him. At the moment you put your trust in God, he comes to live within your spirit. This is the beginning of your process of learning how to love him. My question to you is this: Have you made that faith commitment to God?

Going Deeper

Now let's take a deeper look into the idea of what it means to love God. Have you ever thought seriously about how you think about and treat your Creator and Savior? Several years ago, I was challenged to think about how I was using God by reading J. B. Phillips's book *Your God Is Too Small*.[1] The description of "closet God" resonated with how I put God out of mind and sight until I have a problem. Do I do that? Yes, at times, I have done that.

Among Phillips's other ideas of our small concepts of God is to think of him as a grandfatherly, bearded old gentleman who sits in heaven doing nothing while the world keeps spinning. In other words, God is unconcerned and not participating in the cosmos he created. These small, inadequate ideas of God are reflected in the foolish, immature, and selfish ways we treat him. We need to get to know the one true God personally. He is much bigger and more loving than any of us can comprehend.

How can you love someone you do not know? I want to know the hearts of people I love. I want to understand their concerns and join them in solving problems. I want to treat people I love with respect and consideration. If I am to love God above all others, I must make an effort to know him. How can I know God so that I can learn how to love him?

God has provided all you need to get to know him. He has taken the initiative to reveal himself, to disclose or make himself known to us in various ways. According to Augustine and other great theologians, God wants us to know him and has created a hunger or desire for himself within us. How does God help us satisfy this hunger?

One way God reveals himself is through his natural creation. God demonstrates his beauty, majesty, power, and faithfulness in the heavens and the earth. The psalmist writes, "The heavens are telling the glory of God; and their expanse is declaring the work of His hands. Day to day pours forth speech. And night to night reveals knowledge" (Ps. 19:1–2).

Our planet is a speck in the Milky Way galaxy. The Milky Way is one of thousands and thousands of galaxies in this vast and seemingly endless universe that our Lord has created! Our God is awesome, wonderful, and beautiful. Daily he reveals himself through what he has made. The more you consider the universe in which you live, the more you will recognize his greatness and love for you. Every day the created order speaks to you about God. Are you listening? What are you learning about him?

Another way in which God makes himself known is through significant people in your life. If you are fortunate, you have gained a sense of who God is in the care and security of a loving home. Your mother and father have served as faithful stewards in caring for your needs and guiding you to know something of God's character. If this has been your good fortune, you have experienced God's faithfulness on an emotional level. God also puts others in your life through whom you can learn about him. I have been very fortunate to have had many wise and caring friends who have invested in me. God can also make himself known through the love of surrogate parents, your spouse, children, friends, mentors, teachers, and many others who know God.

The Bible is a trustworthy source for getting to know God and what is on his heart. It is a collection of sixty-six books which begins with the story of creation in Genesis and culminates with the close of human history in Revelation. You learn about who God is in the Old Testament as he reveals himself in a particular way to Israel and sets them apart to carry out his salvation purpose to all nations. Through the prophets, you see God calling his people to repent and join him in his work to save a lost world. In wisdom literature, you are called to embrace God's wisdom as your way of life. Also, the Old Testament tells you that God has a unique plan to accomplish his purpose of bringing people to himself through a great act of personal sacrifice in the Messiah.

The New Testament or New Covenant tells you even more of who God is. He came to us in human form as Jesus of Nazareth. This "good news" is about the most significant event of human history as God became flesh and revealed himself as a man. The New Testament is about Jesus, and apart from him, there would be no reason for its existence. The whole of the New Testament rests on the fact of God's intervention in human history as a human baby. This child was the unique Son of God who grew into manhood. He taught, healed, forgave sin, and was crucified and raised from the dead three days later. According to the New Testament, he has gone back to heaven and will return to earth to resurrect the dead and bring to heaven all who have put their trust in him.

If you want to know the heart and concern of God, you need to look no further than Jesus. On one occasion, Philip, one of the twelve disciples, asked Jesus to show him and the other disciples what God is like, and Jesus makes this astounding statement: "He who has seen me has seen the Father..." (John 14:8–9).

God's Generous Offer

So with all this in mind, how do I "invest" in God? Another way to ask this question is, "How do I show my love for God? Let's begin by considering God's "offer" to us and the "terms" of this offer.

God offers you the forgiveness of your sin of playing god and living life on your own terms. It may be that you acknowledge God's existence but have not surrendered to his love and put your trust in him. He has provided your forgiveness through the death, burial, and resurrection of Jesus. That is the only offer on the table, and you must choose to accept or reject it. There is no bargaining, no counteroffer. It is nonnegotiable. This is God's plan. There is no other way for you to receive forgiveness and to have a right relationship with God. God will love you even if you decide to stay "lost" from Him, but you will miss out on life's great purpose and will eventually lose your very soul in the process.

What are the conditions for you to take advantage of God's offer? Like other relationships, your relationship with God has the basic elements of knowledge and faith. We learn about God through creation, others, and the scriptures and revelation by the Spirit of God. We come to know God personally by actually believing in, trusting him to make good on his offer to us. Ephesians 2:8 tells us "by grace you have been saved through faith: and that not of yourselves, it is the gift of God." In John 3:16, Jesus said to his nighttime inquirer Nicodemus, "For God so loved the world that he gave His only begotten Son, that whoever believes in Him should not perish, but have eternal life."

These scriptures are two of the many examples in the New Testament of how we are to respond to God's offer of a personal relationship with him. The wisest choice you will ever make is to stop putting your faith in yourself and to place (invest) your faith in God. This faith investment in God is not about making a truce with God. It is complete surrender. He will be God, or he will not be God at all.

You may protest that this is unfair and too narrow a deal for you. But all truth is narrow. 2 + 2 is always 4; it is never 3 or 5. Water doesn't freeze at 33 degrees but at 32. Jesus is your Savior and your way to God. Make that faith investment. This choice will put you on a path to building a life portfolio that will serve you well in time and eternity. By the way, the ROI is unbelievable!

In his book *Crazy Love*, Francis Chan raises the issue of God's priority in our lives with these penetrating questions: "Are you willing to say to God he can have whatever he wants?" "Do you believe that wholehearted commitment to Him is more important than any other thing or person in your life?" And "Do you know that nothing you do in this life will ever matter, unless it is about loving God and loving the people he has made?"[2]

The first step toward loving God is to commit to him and his plan by choosing to trust him. Trusting Jesus as your Savior and living Lord establishes a new relationship with God. He is your Father and you are his child. As you will see in the coming chapters, much of loving God has to do with obeying his teachings about how you are to treat yourself and others.

In *Making Sense of God*,[3] Timothy Keller probes why many people are so discontent and the various ways in which they attempt to make sense of life, to find purpose or the "it" that justifies their existence. To answer this concern, he refers us to the work of Saint Augustine of Hippo, a fourth-century bishop. Augustine had a deep interest in why many people were discontent, lacking a sense of joy in life. Here is my take on the essence of Keller's contentions.

Augustine said there were two reasons for a person's discontentment with life: a functional cause and the ultimate source of our happiness. Augustine believed our character is shaped by what we love. What we love is more powerful to determine our actions than what we say we believe. What we set our affections on is the central issue of life. It is not a problem that we love our spouse, our children, our house, our friends, and so on. The "functional" issue is when we get them out of order. For example, if I love my job more than my family, I begin to neglect them, and ultimately, the relationships deteriorate. If I love my children or spouse more than God, I depend on them to supply my deepest sense of contentment, which they cannot do, and relationships suffer. Bottom line: God has designed a pecking order for the loves of our life, and when they get out of order, we harm ourselves and others.

The ultimate reason for our discontent is the source—what or whom we choose to make us happy. Jesus tells us the only lasting source of joy is God. We are made to know God and to love him above all else. We must love first things first. Our discontentment comes when we put other people or things before God. The failure to love God supremely is idolatry, the underlying reason for our lack of contentment.

Putting God first, loving him above all else is the wisest way to build our life portfolio.

INVESTMENT REVIEW

1. How does loving God supremely affect the way you invest your life?

2. What is the difference between knowing about God and knowing him personally?

3. What are some ways you can get to know God in a personal way?

CHAPTER ELEVEN

Loving Self

You shall love your neighbor as yourself.
—Matthew 22:39

During my teenage and young adult years, I believed being loved by someone special was the most important and fulfilling thing that could happen to me. I dated several girls in high school and college and had a couple of serious relationships before meeting my wife. There was something missing in me that I thought could be fixed by being in love. While looking for that elusive something in a relationship while in college, I shared my concern with a college staff person who took the time to listen. After hearing what I had to say, she gave me some advice that changed my thinking about love. The takeaway piece of wisdom is this: "Focus on how to be a loving person rather than being loved." I've come to realize that she was, in her sweet way, telling me to grow up, to get some character. In essence, she was advising me to change my approach in relation-ships from wanting to be loved to becoming a loving person. This line of thinking took me to an understanding of something about love that I think is often overlooked: the biblical teaching of the importance to love our self.

What Is "Loving Myself" About?

Jesus's teaching and example emphasize that loving God above all else is life's supreme goal. However, he links a second idea to that teaching as being *like it:* "And," he says, "you shall love your neighbor as yourself." Think about what he is saying. First, he makes a direct connection between loving God and loving people. You cannot truly love God and not love people. Love for God will cause you to love others. Second, this love for others comes from within us; its source is a healthy love for ourselves. This implies we cannot love others unless we love ourselves.

What does Jesus mean by suggesting that we are to love ourselves? Is he implying we should always look out for number one? Does he suggest that we use whatever means necessary to get what we want? Our culture tends to answer yes, while Jesus is saying something radically different.

Jesus's teaching on this subject is counter cultural, unlike much of today's thinking about love. He said if we want to follow him, we must "deny" ourselves. How is denying ourselves loving ourselves? And didn't he say that if we want to "save" our life, we must "lose" it? We are to love ourselves but deny ourselves. We are to love ourselves but lose ourselves. How are we to make sense of this?

Think about who you are at the core. The biggest problem for each of us is that we insist on playing god. God will have none of it. He offers the only solution to this problem. As strange as it may sound, we love our self best as we deny that self-centered, rebellious, god-impostor part of us and surrender that self to God. We truly love ourselves as we allow God to save us from ourselves. By dying to self, we live to God. That is what it means to love ourselves.

C. S. Lewis has a very sobering way of putting it: "Christ says, 'Give me all. I don't want so much of your time and so much of your money and so much of your work: I want you…No half measures are any good. I don't want to cut off a branch here and a branch there, I want to have the whole tree down. Hand over the whole self…I will give you a new self instead. In fact I will give you myself: my own will shall become yours.'"[1]

From the Inside Out

What I am describing as the way to love ourselves is painful because the old self fights God and clings to pride and self-advancement. Our need for radical change is so great that God did the most unimaginable thing possible to get our attention and to draw us to himself. He gave his Son as a sacrifice for my sin and yours. Radical love like this demands a drastic change from the inside out.

Our ability to love others begins within us. Only loving people can genuinely love others. And we can become caring people only as we allow God to transform us by his love. The most loving thing I can ever do for myself is to put God first. By putting God first, you learn to love him, and he creates you as a loving person who can show God's love for others. This change of character is your conversion.

Once the commitment to Christ has taken place, God continues the process of gradually making you into the image of Christ. And just as your conversion was a process, so is your spiritual growth. This spiritual growth after conversion is sanctification, the process by which God is refining your character. There may be times when you seem to advance quickly and other periods when you don't notice much improvement at all. You must accept the fact that God knows what he is doing and has a plan tailored to your needs. Your job is to be obedient and allow God to accomplish his work in you.

While working as a therapist, I listened to stories of many people whose self-images were damaged by emotionally wounded parents. Some of these people had a history of severe relationship dysfunctions going back generations. This kind of background makes loving oneself problematic. Healing requires a conversion of thinking about oneself as well as a resolution at a deep emotional level. But there is hope. With appropriate help, God's Spirit can heal and make us into genuinely loving people.

It is essential to realize that God influences but does not eradicate your will at conversion. So you have the choice to live selfishly or to commit to building your character around becoming a loving person. This spiritual approach will involve a commitment to continuous growth as you yield to God in faith and allow him to make you like himself. Paul says in Romans 8 that God intends to make you into the "image of his son." What does it mean that God is changing you to be like Jesus? Stay with me as we approach this question from a couple of different directions.

Cooperating with God's Spirit

The apostle Paul tells us in 1 Corinthians 13:4–6 that the supreme personal quality to strive for is to love as Jesus did. He describes the loving person as acting this way: "Love is patient, love is kind, and is not jealous: love does not brag and is not arrogant, does not act unbecomingly; it does not seek its own, is not provoked, does not take into account a wrong suffered, does not rejoice in unrighteousness, but rejoices with the truth."

Earlier, I made a statement to the effect that when you make that foundational investment of accepting Christ as your Savior, the Spirit of God comes to live within you to begin making you into a loving person. In Galatians 5:22–23, Paul says that the fruit the Spirit produces is love. The Spirit of God who lives within you makes you into a loving person whose attitudes and actions are counter to the world marketplace in which you live: "But the fruit of the Spirit is love, joy, peace, patience, kindness, goodness, faithfulness, gentleness, self-control."

So the beginning to loving yourself is to yield to God and allow him to develop you into a loving person who will, over time, exhibit the character qualities Paul has identified in these biblical passages.

A Balanced Approach to Living

Another way to think about loving ourselves is what Stephen Covey says is the seventh of *The 7 Habits of Highly Effective People.*[2] Habit seven is "Sharpen the Saw." The following story is one I have borrowed from Covey and adapted to illustrate the need to keep ourselves "sharp" for God's use.

As you are walking in a wooded area, you come upon a man who is laboring hard to fell a tree. His shirt is soaked, and drops of sweat are falling from his face. He is so busy that he hardly notices you approach. You speak. "Man, how long have you been at this?" He shakes his head and grunts. "Four or five hours, I guess." "Four or five hours?" you repeat incredulously. "Yes," he retorts. "This is very hard work."

The silence is broken only by the grating of the saw against the tree. After a few seconds, you kindly suggest, "You are worn out. Why don't you take a break and sharpen your saw?"

Looking up at you, he responds in a frustrated tone, "I don't have time to sharpen the saw. I'm too busy working."

Sharpening the saw is about preserving and enhancing the greatest asset you have. Covey's simple story is an excellent reminder to take care of ourselves well because it is through the total person that we love God and others.

Jesus tells us that we are to love God with all our heart, mind, and soul. Is the idea of sharpening the saw basically another way of saying what our sacred scriptures have been telling us for centuries?

Yes, I believe it is. We love ourselves, God, and others best when we keep a healthy balance of the physical, mental, and social/emotional parts of us.

To love yourself is to give proper care and respect to your whole person. God created you "in his own image" (Gen. 1:27), and you are "fearfully and wonderfully made" (Ps. 139:14). While you may think of yourself as having separate parts, the reality is that you don't *have* a soul; you *are* a soul. Your mind, body, and emotions are different aspects of your essential life, your soul. Recognizing this fact, let's look at some ways for you to love the parts of you that make up the whole person you are.

Love Your Body
Are you to love your physical body? Yes, absolutely. The creation story tells us that God created land, sea, sky, birds, animals—all the created order. On the sixth day, he fashioned and breathed life into the human body he had made from the earth! As physical beings, male and female, we are the supreme expression of God's creative power.

God gave male and female bodies the capacity to think, to feel, to work, to reproduce, to know God himself, and to enjoy fellowship with him. In and through these physical bodies, Adam and Eve were to interact with each other and with their Creator. God placed only one restriction on them: they were not to try to play god. We know the rest of the story and have been repeating their sin ever since.

Your body is subject to sickness, disease, and death because of what happened in the Garden of Eden. However, you are to honor your body and use it for the glory of God so long as you live. Someday, God will give you a new body, a resurrected one! In the meantime, Paul tells you to present your body back to God as an act of worship (Rom. 12:1). In another place, he tells you your body is the temple of the Holy Spirit; God lives in your body. What does this imply about the way you respect your body and its well-being?

Your body is a marvelous instrument, a gift from your loving Creator, and you should do whatever you can to keep it healthy. To take this idea seriously means to live with balance and to consider the types of exercise you need; the kinds and amounts of foods, drinks, and other substances you put into your body; and the balance of work and rest needed to keep you at your best. I believe your body is so important that you need to have definite plans and actions to maintain its maximum usefulness. After all, it is God's creation and worthy of your care.

If you are prone to taking your physical body for granted, you may want to consider the following comment: "When you come right down to it, the most incredible creation in the universe is you—with your fantastic senses and strengths, your ingenious defense systems, and mental capabilities so great you can never use them to the fullest. Your body is a structural masterpiece more amazing than science fiction."[3]

Your body has four organizational levels: cells, tissue, organs, and systems. It is estimated that your body has between seventy-five to one hundred trillion cells; four kinds of tissues; organs such as your heart, lungs, and kidneys, formed by tissue and serving specialized functions; and ten systems, made up of groups of organs that interact to make your body function properly. Can you identify the ten systems that contribute to your well-being? They are as follows: nervous, endocrine, circulatory, digestive, skeletal, skin, urinary, reproductive, muscular, and respiratory.[4]

Love Your Heart

There is a sense in which your body is the instrument of your will and desires. It responds and is the servant of your mind or heart. It is not possible to honor your body if you don't also love your mind.

The mind or heart is the center of our thinking, decision-making functions, as well as the deeper issues of will and convictions. As Jesus said, it is the source of how we do life: "The good man out of the good treasure of his heart brings forth what is good; and the evil man out of the evil treasure brings forth what is evil: for his mouth speaks from that which fills his heart" (Luke 6:45).

How can you love or respect this incredible gift of mind that God has given you? My response is similar to what I have said about loving your body: exercise and proper nourishment.

The Bible often uses the terms *mind*, *heart*, and *soul* interchangeably to indicate the center for our decision-making capacity. The thinking, understanding, reflective, and decision processes take place in the mind. Do you see how critical it is to feed the mind good information, wise counsel? As they say, "Garbage in, garbage out." You have likely heard the saying, "We are what we eat." It is no less true that you are what you put into your mind.

Your mind is the receptacle of what comes through your senses of taste, smell, touch, hearing, and sight. I also believe we receive messages from the enemy, Satan. As your brain works to process information, your mind is evaluating it as valuable or as trash. What determines that evaluation? One factor is the degree of spiritual wisdom or ignorance that you have acquired. The other is the choice you make about what to do with the information at that particular moment. Of course, you can believe something is wrong and destructive and choose to do it anyway.

Let's take pornography as an example. If you allow yourself to watch porn or seek it out, you are putting into your mind information that sexually excites you and treats the persons in those materials as objects. Sexual desire is a gift from God, but the exploitation of another person is wrong by biblical standards. Jesus said that to look at a woman to lust after her is to commit adultery in your heart. Many who study this particular issue warn that putting porn into your mind can result in an addiction that can distort your soul and control your life. My therapeutic work with folks over many years confirms the reason for this concern.

The mind or heart is the central force of your life, and you must take care to put into your mind information to help you live wisely. Holy Scripture is the best source of that wisdom known to man and is the basis of truth by which we evaluate the ideas which are to govern our life. As John McArthur has said, "The Bible is the touchstone to which all truth claims should be brought and by which all other truth must finally be measured."[5]

You love your mind when you make a consistent effort to saturate it with the biblical principles that build good character. If you settle for a lazy mind, you will probably fall for almost any information a politician, preacher, or proponent espousing many of today's cultural values may spout at you. That is a disgrace and a slap in the face of the great Creator, who gave you a mind. Use it. Train it in wisdom and develop your character so you will be able to follow Christ well and enjoy the benefits God intended for you when he gave you a mind.

Love Your Feelings

As a soul, you have a mind with which you think, choose, and act through your body. Your soul also has a broad range of feelings or emotions, which are a source of energy to carry out the tasks of everyday living. Anger, happiness, sadness, and empathy are gifts from God and intended to help you love him, yourself, and others. However, as you may have discovered, your feelings flow from your thinking, and that can be very dangerous. To love yourself well, you must discipline and use your feelings wisely.

One challenge you may have with your feelings is that you can allow them to have control over you. These out-of-control emotions can cause you to act in ways or say things contradictory to the love that should characterize your speech and actions. Feelings are an excellent servant but a terrible master.

Perhaps the most problematic of all feelings is anger, stirred in us when someone or something frustrates our plans, cuts us off in traffic, crosses boundaries, treats us poorly, or insults us. Anger is a great gift from God, and our world would be a miserable place without it. Is that crazy? Not at all—much of the great music and many of the scientific breakthroughs and recoveries from personal disasters have resulted from anger under control. But like all God's gifts, anger is very destructive when not under the control of a genuinely loving mind.

Where do you start to love this emotional part of yourself? Several years ago, I ran across an old book that has been enormously helpful to me: *Understanding Your Emotional Problems,*[6] by Peter Fletcher. I suggest you read this or a similar book to understand the vital role your feelings play in your overall health and how you can use them well. Get to know this part of yourself. You and others will greatly benefit if you will learn to love this part of yourself well.

If you are currently depressed or having other issues with your feelings, consult a good therapist who can help you navigate your concerns by using the resources of your faith to bring about wholeness to your life. Many have found that seeking this kind of help has put them back in charge of their feelings and deepened their relationship with God.

Another thing you can do is admit what you are feeling. Problems tend to occur when we swallow or repress our feelings. To admit you are angry is not a sin. Sin happens when you act inappropriately on that anger. Admit your feeling by saying something like, "I get angry when he does that." Then take the next step and ask yourself, "Why do I get angry when he does that?" Answering this question allows your mind to understand the feeling. Give yourself time to consider what it is about the situation that triggers your anger. This process slows you down from reacting badly and allows you to consider what—if anything—you should do. Then, choose an appropriate response to the situation guided by the biblical principles that you have been feeding your mind.

There is one other thing I want you to consider doing for yourself: get into the habit of journaling several times a week. Writing allows you to get thoughts and feelings outside yourself and helps you see what is subconsciously going on. Keeping a journal is a great and inexpensive way to stay in touch with your challenges, hopes, and goals and prayerfully seek God's guidance to live out your faith and minimize the control your feelings have over you.

INVESTMENT REVIEW

1. What is the connection between loving yourself and loving God and others?

2. To what areas of your physical, mental, and emotional health do you need to give more attention?

3. List some steps you are willing to take to love yourself better.

4. Why is loving yourself sometimes a painful process?

CHAPTER TWELVE

Loving Others

A new commandment I give to you, that you love one another, even as I have loved you, that you also love one another.
—John 13:34

How do we find a healthy balance in our culture? We live with daily tension between our culture's lure to self-centeredness and our calling to be "salt and light" in a world that is desperately looking for love in all the wrong places. Paul encourages us to apply the teachings of Christ in our culture rather than to be shaped by its values.

In his letter to the Philippians, he tells us to live out our salvation experience in our current environment of unbelief and opposition: "Work out your salvation with fear and trembling...in the midst of a crooked and perverse generation, among whom you appear as lights in the world" (Phil. 2:12, 15).

I believe a large part of our struggle in following Paul's instruction is our confusion between the goal of life and the counterfeit offers of our culture. Maybe we are so busy with the "means" that we haven't thought deeply about the "end" or purpose of our existence. A few seem to get it, but many do not. God has intended that our money, time, health, and all good things he has made available to us are to serve as a means to an end. When we forget where these gifts originate or the purpose for which they exist, we become very narrowly focused and selfish. If we follow the way of our culture, our possessions will inevitably possess us.

The Definitive Test of Love

It's time to talk about the third and most character-revealing investment we are called on to make as followers of Jesus. So far, we have considered the initial and most crucial investment of commitment to Christ as well as the investment into becoming a loving person. We have discovered that it is God's goal to make us into new people who act like Christ in our culture. The third investment is "where the rubber hits the road." How we treat others is the definitive test of who we are and what we truly believe.

As a reminder of what the bottom line is about, let's look one more time at what Jesus said about the ultimate meaning of life: "You shall love your neighbor as yourself" (Matt. 22:39). Jesus is telling us the real proof that we love God is how we treat others. Something is drastically wrong if we say we love God and do not love people. John, one of Jesus's disciples, puts the issue this way: "We love because he first loved us. If someone says 'I love God' and hates his brother, he is a liar; for the one who does not love his brother whom he has seen cannot love God whom he has not seen. And this commandment we have from Him, that the one who loves God should love his brother also" (1 John 4:19–21).

Love, seeking what is in the long-term best interest for another, is what makes us most like God. Love motivates God to save us. Love acted on our behalf in the incarnation, death, burial, and resurrection of Jesus: "For God so loved the world…" Love works in the best interest of the beloved.

When the apostle John wrote the words above in 1 John, he was likely reflecting on an experience where Jesus spoke directly to him and the other disciples about the vital connection between loving God and our treatment of others. With the disciples gathered around the table on the night before his crucifixion, Jesus looks at each of them and says, "A new commandment I give to you, that you love one another, even as I have loved you, that you also love one another. By this all men will know that you are my disciples if you have love for one another" (John 13:34–35).

Do you say you love Jesus and want to follow him? He welcomes you and me with open arms and tells us, "If you love me, you will keep my commandments" (John 14:15).

Love Means Investing

To follow Jesus is to invest our lives in others. Who are the "others" we are to love, and what does it mean to love them? There is an encounter recorded in Luke 10:25–37 that will help answer these questions. In this conversation, the questioner asks Jesus what a person must do to inherit eternal life. Jesus answers his question with a couple of his own: "What is written in the law? How does it read to you?" The man responds by quoting the Great Commandment, and Jesus follows that up with this challenge: "You have answered correctly; do this and you will live."

But the inquirer is not finished. "And who is my neighbor?" Does the inquirer really want an answer, or is he testing Jesus? Whatever the case, Jesus is going to tell him a story he will not soon forget. The story he is about to tell is about the messy, unpleasant reality of life and how love responds. It is easy to say, "I love you," to even think we love, but what we do is the real test. The man's question, "Who is my neighbor?" sets the stage for one of the greatest stories Jesus ever told, the one we know as the Parable of the Good Samaritan.

It is a profoundly meaningful story, couched in simple words about a familiar happening along the road between Jerusalem and Jericho. A man is traveling this dangerous passage when robbers jump him. They beat him and rob him and leave him to die. Their actions show total disregard for several of the commandments God gave to Moses. They have sinned greatly by what they have done. They have no mercy on him. It would be bad enough if the story ends here, but it doesn't. No...the story takes a turn that may implicate the very man who began this discussion with Jesus.

You see, the questioner is a person who knew Old Testament scriptures. And the two persons who become Jesus's next characters in the story are also very religious people, a priest and a Levite. These two would naturally ascribe to the basic teachings of Judaism. They were more than just modern-day churchgoers. They were the most religious of the religious. But there is a problem that can affect even the most religious among us. They have a blind spot, a strong disconnect between their head and their heart, between their type of religion and the countercultural gospel Jesus came preaching about loving others. So what did these religious folks do when they came upon this wounded stranger in dire need? Nothing. That's correct. They did nothing to help him. They were so busy being religious and "serving" God that they squelched any tug of compassion and went on their way. They broke the first commandment about loving God; they didn't love this person in need.

This story is a strong caution to anyone interested in doing good for God. Our faith and organized religion are empty and useless when they exist to promote ourselves or to keep a dead organization going. True religion is not about us and our goals. It is about demonstrating our love for Christ, our Savior, by offering what help we can to those in need.

The fate of the dying man depends on someone who will have mercy on him. Fortunately, another traveler is on his way. This person will be the hero, the true believer in the story.

So who is this true believer? Enter a Samaritan. There is no question that Jesus's choice of a Samaritan was intended to shock this self-righteous Jew. Could a half-breed, despised by many Jews, be more attuned with God than the very religious Jews? The answer to this question is evident in the Samaritan's compassionate actions. He is blind to race, religion, social status, or politics. Here is one man made in the image of God, seeing another person made in the image of God in pressing need. His compassion takes over.

And so the story goes. The Samaritan cleans the man's wounds, brings him to where he can get additional help, and promises to cover any further expense incurred. What human kindness he shows to this stranger in need! This kind of love is inconvenient, dirty, and expensive. True love always costs us something.

To end this stunning exchange, Jesus looks into the somber eyes of the inquirer and asks, "Which of the three do you think proved to be a neighbor to the man who fell into robbers' hands?" Sobered by what he has just heard, the lawyer replies, "The one who showed mercy toward him." Remember what prompted this story. The discussion started with a question about how to get eternal life. It ends with Jesus's simple instruction: "Go and do the same."

Where Do You Start?

The Bible tells us that God loves everyone. There are over seven billion people living today, over 330 million in the United States and over 500 million in North America. How can I possibly love all these people? You can't be physically present for everyone. You don't have the financial resources to heal all the wounds in the world either. You can't be everywhere at once, and you don't have the time to be there, even if you could. Only God can love all these people, but we can love those whom God puts in our daily lives.

The Samaritan's heart prompted his compassionate actions toward the wounded stranger. His hands, feet, and words became instruments of the deep respect he had for the life of another human being. Respect is the key to loving the whole world. Respecting the sacredness of another human being is the starting place to loving a cantankerous neighbor who allows his dog to poop in your yard. How do you see people—a nuisance, a means to your ends? Do you consider them as individuals with feelings and needs like your own? Do you treat all people with respect regardless of their race, sexual orientation, political affiliation, or social status?

We encounter nameless people daily at the post office or supermarket and on the crowded highways. How do we love them? Perhaps your love for a stranger can be shown by opening a door for the person with an armful of packages or by allowing that person with one item to go ahead of you. Or maybe you can show love for that family of four going on vacation by not endangering their lives by driving while intoxicated, texting, or driving recklessly. Loving people, in general, boils down to using good judgment and a bit of courtesy, common sense, and kindness.

Love involves imagination, the work of thinking about how what we do and say may affect others. It is a habit everyone needs to develop. Jesus tells us to love all people, including our enemies. When power or something other than love is the endgame, everyone loses, whether it is politics, family life, business, or your local congregation.

Our culture needs a radical change that only the gospel can give. Husbands, wives, children, siblings, employers, employees, religious leaders, and so on are the source of the sorely dysfunctional relationships that permeate our culture. Christ can give us a new heart, one that respects the personhood of others.

A significant part of loving others well is to understand where our boundaries stop and the other person's boundaries begin. What would happen in our world if we began attempting to live by the Ten Commandments? The commandments are rules about living within healthy limits. The first four rules define our relationship between our Creator and us. The boundaries include the exclusive worship of God, reverence for who he is, and the keeping of the Sabbath to worship him and rest. These boundaries define what we often call the vertical dimension of relationships—God to man. The later six rules pertain to the horizontal relationships between human beings—how we are to treat each other.

In their monumental work *Boundaries*, Cloud and Townsend say, "We are responsible to others and for ourselves...Denying ourselves to do for others what they cannot do for themselves is showing the sacrificial love of Christ...This is being responsible 'to.'"[1]

Being responsible *to* others involves respect for positional, personal, and property boundaries. Treating our parents with due care and respect is at the top of the list of the later six rules for a reason. Learning to love ourselves and others begins with respecting our parents. A child's healthy respect for his parents is critical to his good emotional development. It is also the foundation for building a loving, caring character.

A respectful relationship with our parents begins a natural progression of how we are to relate to others. Here's how that works. We are to honor the sanctity of life of another person, forbidden to murder anyone. We are to respect the boundary that sexual intercourse is limited to the marriage of a man and woman. Love for others draws a line between what is their property and what is ours. Taking something that isn't ours without permission is not allowed. We are to be respectful of the reputations and characters of others by not lying or distorting information that can harm them in any way. Don't lie about people. The final commandment sets a boundary on our attitude or desire concerning something belonging to someone else: car, house, wife, husband, or lifestyle. To *covet* means to want what does not belong to you. It is an attitude or desire that makes you miserable and is just an act away from sinning against someone else.

You may have noticed the Ten Commandments and other statements of law in the Old Testament tend to come across as prohibitions: "Thou shall not." Although Jesus grew up immersed in the Old Testament scriptures, he has a noticeably refreshing approach in his application of the law and the prophets. He tells us that acting out of love will take away any incentive to violate the boundaries of other people. With that in mind, see what an investment in loving others might look like in everyday living.

Five Things You Can Do to Love Others

So how can you express love in the way you treat others? Here are some different ways you can use your life and gifts to love others. Daily living at home, in the office, at lunch with a friend, and in chance meetings can offer opportunities to be helpful to others.

Love through your words. Have you considered how you use your words? Words can have a powerful effect on people for good or evil. Our words are important, and we are responsible for how we use them with others. That is why Jesus cautions us, "Every careless word that men shall speak, they shall render account for it in the day of judgment" (Matt. 12:36).

With this caution in mind, let me mention a test we can use before we speak to or about another person. If our words meet the three strict criteria, they will express wisdom and love. First, is what you are about to say *true*? If you are sure you know the truth, consider the next question: Is it *helpful*? Just because something is true doesn't mean you have to say it. Check the intent of your heart before you say something that could bring hurt or embarrassment to someone. If you say something that you know to be true, let it also come from the motive to be helpful. Paul reminds us that we are to carefully check our motivation when speaking a difficult truth to someone: "Speak the truth in love" (Eph. 4:15). If what you want to say has cleared these two hurdles, expose it to one more: Is it *necessary*? The question is very practical. Does what you intend to say help the situation? Is it critical information that needs to be shared? It is only necessary if it is true and helpful.

It seems much of what we hear and read today comes through no filters at all. Deliberately lying or "spinning" information to further a personal or political agenda seems to be tolerated in lots of public discourse today. Our words are important, and what we say and why we say it reveals our character. Words can honor Christ if we are careful to use them to show compassion and care for others.

Sometimes I make a note in my daily to-do list to say something to encourage someone whom God may bring to my mind. Everyone needs an encouraging word from time to time, and I believe being proactive or deliberate about this is a loving way to use our words to help a fellow human being.

Proverbs 15:23 says, "How delightful is a timely word." I know this to be true because many caring people have spoken encouraging and helpful words into my life. When I was discouraged or struggling to find my way, God put an encourager in my path to restore my hope. I remember a phone call from a friend when I was very lonely and in a career crisis. I was encouraged that he took the time to check on me. His words lifted my spirit and helped me get on with what I needed to do. That friend died several years ago, but his words and the act of encouragement continue to live in me.

A friendly hello to a stranger may be the boost they need. An encouraging word to a friend or family member could change a day or a lifetime. A timely text, phone call, or email can remind someone you care about and remember them in their trial. Words matter. Allow the wisdom of Psalm 19:14 to guide you as you consider how to love others with your words: "Let the words of my mouth and the meditation of my heart be acceptable in Thy sight, O Lord, my rock and my redeemer."

Love through your influence. Who has influenced your life? The power of my mother's influence kept me from many stupid mistakes in my teenage years. Oh, I did my share of risky things, but the very thought of displeasing her kept me from sins that I would remember in later years. The only thing that came close to a lecture from her was the caution to "watch who you are friends with." She was concerned, and rightly so, that hanging out with a wrong crowd would influence me to do things I shouldn't do. Although I had the freedom to act, she had this power or influence that caused me to be careful about how far I would go down the road of stupidity. Her love for the Bible and the way she lived caused me to want to do well. Her life and influence were, no doubt, significant influences on my decision to become a Christian. My mother and several others have had a tremendous impact on my life for good. Likewise, I want my life to have a positive, godly influence on my family, friends, and others God may put in my life.

To have a good influence on others, we must be sure to choose our influencers well. Do you seek out the wisdom of others? Do you read the scriptures and allow the Holy Spirit to guide you to understand and apply biblical teachings to your life?

We have a choice about what or who we allow to influence us. Some who profess to follow Christ have chosen to be influenced by alcohol, drugs, pornography, or some diversion that alters their thinking and acting. Paul offers a strong caution about such issues in Ephesians 5:18: "And do not get drunk with wine, for that is dissipation, but be filled with the Spirit." The Holy Spirit and scripture will never mislead you. Let them teach you the way of Christ as you, in turn, seek to be a positive influence on others. And remember, the fruit of the Spirit is love. Following his leadership will help you become a loving influence on those around you.

As followers of Jesus, we are called on to be "salt and light" in our culture. Salt and light are symbols for influencers or change agents. Light dispels darkness, and salt gives flavor. While we cannot and should not try to usurp another person's right to choose, we can attempt to influence their decisions by how we live. Jesus is very clear about how we should be intentional to influence others by the way we conduct our life: "Let your light shine before men in such a way that they may see your good works and glorify your Father who is in heaven" (Matt. 5:16).

Do you have children? If so, they observe whether or not you keep promises. They see whether you attempt to live by what you profess. Small children tend to believe their parents are almost perfect and want to be like them. Whether or not you intend for your actions to influence your child is not the issue. The fact is that your actions do have an influence on the most important people in your life. The question is: What kind of influence will you be?

Think about the power of your influence in the way you use your time, how you take care of your health, the way you manage finances, and other resources God has placed under your management. Consider how you treat people. Do you make differences in the way you respect your boss and the clerical worker? Is your language acceptable for your children to emulate? Your influence is like a type of infectious disease that you spread to your spouse and children, at work, at church, and among friends. For good or bad, you are influencing people every day.

I once attended a funeral where the minister described the character of the deceased in a way that was unrecognizable as that of the person who had been alive a few days before. How we treat others indicates the nature of our character. Some day someone will say the last words over you. What will they say if they tell the truth?

You have the opportunity to love others through the influence or impact your life can have on them. Just as the character and values of those who have loved you continue to influence you, the way you live can have a tremendous impact on family members and others long after you are gone. We die, but our influence lives on.

Love through giving. The tone of this book may have left you with the impression that money is not important. Allow me to be perfectly frank. Money is important. The problem with money comes when we misunderstand its purpose and elevate it to the priority of our life. The Bible doesn't teach that being rich is wrong if we have acquired wealth through honest means.

The scriptures have lots to say about money because it has such power for good or evil. However, the Bible does warn us about putting our trust in wealth because that is idolatry. Our society worships at the altar of wealth. It can easily become one's god, his security, his power, and purpose for living. We must keep perspective on the primary purpose of our life. To that end, the apostle Paul shares a concern with a younger friend that we will be wise to consider:

> But godliness actually is a means of great gain, when accompanied by contentment. For we have brought nothing into the world, so we cannot take anything out of it either. And if we have food and covering, with these we shall be content. But those who want to get rich fall into temptation and a snare and many foolish and harmful desires which plunge men into ruin and destruction. For the love of money is a root of all sorts of evil, and some by longing for it have wandered away from the faith and have pierced themselves with many a pang. But flee from these things, you man of God; and pursue righteousness,

godliness, faith, love, perseverance and gentleness
(1 Tim. 6:6–11).

The desire to accumulate wealth can be a problem for anyone—
male, female, rich, or poor. As Paul says, "Those who desire to get
rich fall into temptation and a snare." We should strive for godliness
and contentment, whether God has blessed us with little or much.

How can your money and possessions become a means of loving others? Whether you have much or little, you are expected to
be a good manager of what you have. Loving others through our
money involves attitudes and actions.

First, we need to agree with the biblical teaching that everything belongs to God. What we possess has a time limit; it is ours
to use for only a while. Second, we are to show gratitude to God
for his provisions and care for our needs. Third, we need to develop an attitude of contentment, which is a seemingly rare thing
in our culture. It is not sinful to want to earn more, but we must
keep our priorities in order and not strive for wealth to hoard it or
make it the source of our security. Fourth, God wants us to give
like he does: cheerfully and without a grudging or stingy spirit.
In 2 Corinthians 9:6–7, Paul instructs believers concerning the
generous attitude that should motivate our giving: "Now this I say,
he who sows sparingly shall also reap sparingly; and he who sows
bountifully shall also reap bountifully. Let each one do just as he
has purposed in his heart; not grudgingly or under compulsion;
for God loves a cheerful giver."

The Old Testament references a tithe as the recognition that
everything belongs to God. While God doesn't need anything we
have, the act of giving regularly and generously is for our good. It
reminds us that we are dependent on God for all we have. The New
Testament doesn't negate this teaching but emphasizes the importance of our attitude in giving. Jesus calls attention to this while he

and the disciples observed an occasion where people were making their gifts in the collection area at the temple. A poor widow has only two small coins and willingly gives them to the service of the Lord. It is all she has. The well-to-do are also there and give much more than the poor widow. Jesus assesses what happened this way: "This poor widow put in more than all the contributors to the treasury; for they all put in out of their surplus, but she, out of her poverty, put in all she owned, all she had to live on" (Mark 12:43–44).

There are many excellent organizations, including your church, that want your money. Once you give it to one, it seems many others have a way of finding out about you. As a good manager, you will want to be prayerful and check out the organization to which you give. Beyond that, be generous to others and see how God will grow you to be more lavishly generous like your Father.

Money has power, and we need to be judicious in how and to whom we give. Because money has the potential to help or harm, I want to offer a caution. Everyone likes to receive, but our giving can be harmful if it fosters a lifestyle of irresponsibility or laziness. It is unloving to give if doing so supports an attitude of entitlement. One of the most challenging issues in parenting is to provide for our children without spoiling them. Is it wise to give them everything they want because we can?

Perhaps you may know adults who have the idea that others should take care of them. I have had encounters with people who wanted me to give them money, but when I proposed they help me with some work, their need suddenly went away. At other times the person in need was happy to take some responsibility for earning money. Allow compassion and wisdom to be your general approach to your giving.

What I have just stated does not apply to every situation, and there are times where people need help immediately. We cannot always know the motive of the person, but it is still best to err on the side of generosity. The point I'm attempting to make is to give in an attitude of care to help and not harm the person through the gift.

The book of James has lots to say about how real faith in God is shown by our works—how we treat others. "If a brother or sister is without clothing and in need of daily food, and one of you says to him, 'Go in peace, be warmed and be filled,' and yet you do not give them what is necessary for their body, what use is that?" (James 2:16–17).

While being generous with our possessions helps others, it also makes us more like God.

Love through prayer. I have prayed all my life. I have prayed all kinds of prayers, from the simple "Now I lay me down to sleep" prayer of my early childhood to prayers of praise and thanksgiving as I wandered the fields and hills of the farm where I grew up. I have prayed very ignorant and selfish prayers. I have prayed tearful prayers and joyful prayers. I have prayed for forgiveness and guidance.

How prayer works is a mystery to me. That mystery is never explicitly explained in the Bible. There is an unspoken assumption in both testaments that there is an innate need for people to petition God; prayer is considered a vital part of faithful living.

Some of the most poignant and moving prayers are those of David in the Psalms. There are also prayers by Moses, Abraham, Jacob, Jabez, Samuel, Elijah, and many others. John the Baptist taught his followers to pray, and Jesus has given us an outline or model for prayer. There are numerous examples in the New Testament of Jesus praying or teaching about prayer. Prayer is a big deal.

As I have matured a bit, I have become more aware of the absolute necessity of a kind of prayer that focuses on the needs of someone else. It is a prayer I can offer about their struggles, pain, need for guidance, healing of relationships, or areas of growth. God cares about everything that concerns them, and I can love them by praying for them. This kind of prayer is an excellent way to love other people. It is called intercessory prayer—praying to God on their behalf.

Praying for the good of someone else is a real act of love. It joins me with them to see God's purpose done in their life. Praying for another person takes time and effort and is as much an act of love as anything we can do for them. Prayer can also open our hearts to consider how God can use us to answer our prayer for them. God's concern is that all people come to experience his forgiveness and grow in the likeness of Christ. When we pray for God's will in another person's life, we are agreeing with God's purpose for them and allowing his Spirit to love them through us.

Our Lord's intercessory prayer for those who crucified him is the epitome of selfless love and consistent with his insistence that we pray for our enemies. Let his compassion for others remind you of how you are to love others by praying for them, "Father forgive them: for they do not know what they are doing" (Luke: 23:34).

A prayer list helps me remember to pray for others regularly. My list includes my family members, friends, neighbors, church leaders, various ministries, military personnel and their families, and local, state, and national leaders. I can make adjustments to the list as needed. Other than helping guide whom to pray for, the list also serves to remind me to reach out to others and not be consumed with praying only for myself. It is a practical tool to help me love other people.

Of course, interceding for others is not confined to the list or to a specific time of day. Interceding for others can also be spontaneous as the Spirit brings something or someone to my consciousness. What a beautiful thing it is to be able to join with God's work in loving people as we pray for his will on their behalf. Such praying not only helps them, but it also expands our hearts and makes us more like our Lord.

Love through listening. I have spent a good part of my professional life listening to people talk about their concerns. On the surface, it would seem that listening is an easy thing to do. However, I have discovered that deep listening is some of the most challenging and exhausting work I have ever done. I think you will agree with me about that if you have ever taken listening to someone else really seriously. Listening is vital to healthy relationships and is a skill every follower of Christ should seek to develop.

Communication is an essential component of all our significant relationships. I would dare say that most failed marriages share a common thread of a lack of understanding and trust, which are built only when two people work hard at communicating well. Listening is a crucial part of communication. All our important relationships suffer when we fail at listening well.

To love another person well, we must accept and understand them. Deep relationships are not the product of wishful thinking or magic. Neither are they produced by judging and trying to "fix" the other person. Those you are trying to love will be inclined to be vulnerable with you about personal concerns, anxieties, and dreams if they know they can trust you. How can you help them trust you with their feelings and concerns? Listen without judging or trying to fix them or the issue.

You may think you are listening when you are only hearing. There is a big difference between the two. You must be able to hear to listen, but listening and hearing are not the same. Hearing depends on the physical ability to discern sounds. Listening is attempting to understand the meaning of the sounds the other person is making.

Surely you have experienced the difference between being listened to and being heard. It is highly probable that you have been on both sides of such situations. Recall a time when you believed the other person attempted to listen to you. How did you feel? How did you think this experience helped you? Now, can you recall a situation when you were trying to have a conversation, and the other person was distracted, or their attention was diverted by something else? When someone continues to repeat this behavior, relationships decline, disappear, or remain stuck where they are.

Not all conversations require deep listening. Some are more surface and require less effort, but it is a good thing to listen well in these times as well in order to establish a pattern of trust, which can lead to a deeper relationship. Good listening tells me you care about me and the things that are happening in my life. When you listen to me, it means you have put your immediate needs and concerns on hold and are investing yourself in me. It is one of the best ways I know to say, "I love you." I have enjoyed this kind of love from many people in my life, and it is a life-changing experience.

What is required of you to be an active, loving listener? In my book *Marriage Is What You Make It*,[2] I make some suggestions about being a "focused listener" that apply to all healthy relationships. Focused listening involves paying close attention to what someone is saying and how they are saying it. Listening is difficult work, but the payoff is enormous. Here are some tips you may want to consider:

- Make a strong effort to hear what the other person is trying to say.

- Minimize all external distractions by turning off the TV, radio, phone, and so forth so you can pay attention.

- Turn down the internal distractions. Calm your mind and emotions by taking a deep breath to relax or use some other calming technique to enable you to listen.

- Compartmentalize or momentarily put aside concerns that may interfere with your ability to listen. If you are distracted by your project or what is next on your agenda, you cannot focus on what the other person is saying. When a critical discussion is taking place, don't allow anything but an emergency to disrupt it.

- Hold yourself accountable for listening well. If you allow yourself to become distracted, apologize and ask the person to repeat what was said. Doing this will serve as a good discipline for you and will convey to the other person you are trying to listen to.

- Wait for your turn to talk. Avoid interrupting, arguing, correcting, or formulating your response until you are sure you have heard what was said.

- Pay attention to nonverbal communication that is taking place. The tone of voice, facial expressions, and body language give additional information about the importance of what the person is saying. Words are the basics of the "communication soup," but the nonverbal elements can be the spices that give the soup a lot of its flavor.

- Test how well you listen. When the other person has come to a stopping point, repeat or summarize what you have heard. Allow the person to correct any misunderstanding and continue the process until it is your turn to respond.

- Consider the importance of your listening presence. Sometimes we need to be present with people who are hurting, and there is nothing we can or should say to fix the situation. Your presence and listening ear is what they need. Allow them to talk, but do not feel the need to say something "spiritual" to comfort them. Your presence and care are the spiritual help they need. Just be there and listen.

Listening well is not easy, but it is essential to build understanding. For most people, feeling understood is closely akin to feeling loved.

For many, the prayer of Saint Francis of Assisi demonstrates the heart and attitude of the Christ-follower who sincerely seeks to live out the gospel in a world that rewards pride, selfishness, and the objectification of others. Read it and think of what our culture would be like if everyone aspired to its challenge.

The Prayer of Saint Francis
Lord, make me an instrument of your peace.
Where there is hatred, let me sow love.
Where there is injury, pardon.
Where there is despair, hope.
Where there is darkness, light.
And, where there is sadness, joy.
O divine master, grant that I may
Not so much seek to be consoled as to console,
To be understood as to understand,
To be loved as to love.
For it is in giving that we receive.
It is in pardoning that we are pardoned.
And it is in dying that we are born into eternal life.
Amen[3]

INVESTMENT REVIEW

1. What is your greatest challenge to "love others"?

2. Evaluate this statement: how we treat others is the real measure of how much we love Jesus. See Matthew 22:39 and John 4:19–21.

3. What is God teaching you about how loving others relates to his plan for your life?

4. What does respecting the personal boundaries of others have to do with loving them?

5. You can use words, influence, giving, praying, and listening as some of the ways you can love others. Recall how someone has used one of these to show love for you. What will you do to be more intentional in using one or more of these ideas to love others?

PART THREE

Extraordinary Investment Opportunities

CHAPTER THIRTEEN

Becoming One in Marriage

*Husbands, love your wives, just as Christ loved the
church and gave himself up for her...and let the wife see
to it that she respect her husband.*
—Ephesians 5:25, 33

This scripture and many others express the great value God places on marriage. God ordained marriage as the means of propagating the human race. Loving marriages provide children with solid foundations for life and bolster the health of the general society.

There is no greater test of love among human beings than the devotion required in marriage. In Ephesians 5, the apostle Paul emphasizes the selfless, sacrificial love that marriage demands by comparing it to Christ's relationship to his bride, the church. What Christ did to redeem us sets the standard for the way husbands and wives are to treat each other.

Marriage Is What You Make It

While the marriage relationship is critically important to society, it is also tremendously vulnerable because of factors within society, as well as the challenges inherent in marriage itself. God's intention for the physical and spiritual union of a man and woman in marriage requires commitment and hard work. Too often, people embark on this venture without the slightest idea of what is involved in building a functional marriage. Many marriages end in divorce, and some are stuck in an unhealthy relationship because they are naive, afraid, immature, or just too lazy to do the work required in a good marriage.

Some people seem to think of marriage as a type of magical box. Inside that box are happiness, fulfillment, personal satisfaction, success, and fairy dust that assure a blissful "happily ever after" marriage. The truth is that the "magical" box is an empty box that you must fill with love, patience, endurance, kindness, selflessness, compromise, and many other grown-up kinds of qualities. Your marriage will be what both of you put into the box.[1]

I prefer the term *functional* rather than *happy* to describe God's intention for marriage. I realize this word doesn't conjure up warm feelings, but I think it more accurately describes what I believe God intends for our marriages. Why? I believe there is a tendency in our culture to promote personal happiness as the goal of our existence. We are obsessed with being happy. We want people and things to make us happy. I believe in happiness and happy marriages. However, real and lasting happiness is not the goal of life but the result or by-product of something else. Because happiness is not the goal in life, I should not expect my marriage or my spouse to supply my joy. Good marriages are not always happy, joyful, or harmonious. Functional marriages are often happy, but there are times when they aren't. People who have happiness as their goal for marriage are often disillusioned and look to someone else to make them happy. Marriage just doesn't accommodate that kind of immaturity.

Think about what the terms *function* and *functional* actually mean. The function of a person, thing, or marriage has to do with the *why* or purpose of their existence. Many marital problems are the result of unrealistic expectations one or both of the partners have related to the purpose of marriage.

My personal and professional experiences have yielded some understanding about how to build a loving relationship with your spouse that will honor God as you fulfill His purpose in your marriage. What makes for a functional marriage?

Many years of counseling couples with a variety of marital concerns and my marriage of a half-century have convinced me that most issues acquiesce when three things are present: commitment, communication, and creative conflict. By doing these three things consistently well, you can build a sense of oneness and also enjoy a good deal of personal happiness in your marriage. Paying attention to these three areas is another way to say those three words (*I love you*) your spouse needs to hear often.

Commitment

"Commitment is continuing to do what you said you would do when the feeling you had when you said it is gone." I don't remember where I saw this statement, but I believe there is a lot of truth in it. Feelings can change, but commitment weathers the storm of emotions. In good times and bad times, I remain committed to my marriage. When I don't feel like it, when I don't particularly like my spouse, I stay and fight for my marriage. My marriage takes precedence over every human relationship and everything else in my life.

Commitment is foundational to a functional marriage. Attempting to make a marriage without commitment is like trying to build a house without a foundation to support it. Devotion to God and his purpose for marriage and each other will see you through the storms that come to every marriage. Commitment also strengthens you during the abundant years when you are tempted to forget God.

Commitment, not feelings, is the determining factor in a good marriage. Functional relationships are not predicated on our feelings at the moment. They are built on a resolve of character to love my marriage enough to allow myself to be changed and do whatever I can to make it what God has intended it to be.

How do you know if you are committed to your marriage? The same way you know you are committed to anything. The level of our commitment is commensurate with the amount of effort we make to what we are trying to accomplish—golf, career, fishing, entertainment, and so on. You are committed to your marriage when you proactively seek ways to grow personally. You are committed if you try to understand your spouse and address ways to meet his or her needs.

The longevity of your marriage is not necessarily an indication of a deep commitment to each other. However, without a deep commitment, marriages do not grow and flourish in the face of the challenges involved in the biblical ideal of "becoming one." Sadly, people can be together for many years and never really know each other well. They may exist together, but they are not one as God has intended.

I have a hunch that marriage may be God's most effective tool for growing believers into the character of Christ. Someone has aptly commented, "A person's character is but half formed till after wedlock."[2] A healthy marriage requires uncommon selflessness, a sacrificial level of love, "just as Christ also loved the Church and gave himself for her" (Eph. 5:25). Commitment involves the choice to seek the well-being of each other, faithfulness to your vows, and the willingness to grow together, building a good marriage together. To love your spouse well will put you on the path to "growing up." And growing up is a significant part of God's plan for you: "For one human being to love another human being: that is perhaps the most difficult task that has been entrusted to us, the ultimate task, the final test and proof, the work for which all other work is merely preparation."[3]

You are certainly aware that you accomplish virtually nothing important in your life without a commitment to cooperate in that endeavor. A good marriage begins with a commitment and deepens and grows as your relationship grows, and new commitments are made to forgive, accept each other, and continue the hard work of becoming one in Christ.

Your marriage vows are not magic. They are a promise that you will stay committed to doing your best to make the marriage work. By God's grace, you will grow through your disagreements; you will learn to fight fairly, speak the truth in love, forgive without being asked to, and consider your spouse's needs more important than your own.

In an earlier section of this book, I related how Brian and Janet had faced the heartbreaking loss of their daughter to suicide. In his response to my questions, Brian shared how someone had predicted that their marriage would not survive the loss of their daughter. Perhaps the person was well-intentioned and had meant his comment as a caution because some marriages do not survive the loss of a child. There are many reasons why marriages fail. Statistics are not predictive of what will happen in individual situations such as that faced by Brian and Janet. Commitment has seen them through their trial. Commitment to God and each other is essential to overcoming life's devastating losses.

Communication

As stated earlier, God's goal for your marriage is for the two of you to become one. What does that mean? How does that happen?

Becoming one implies a sexual relationship in which you and your spouse enjoy the pleasure and release that come as you give yourself to each other physically. This sharing of your physical self is intended to form a deep emotional connection between the two of you. Sexual union is a type of communication that is beyond words. It is body to body, vulnerability to vulnerability. Sexual intercourse can build trust and tenderness toward each other. However, as important as the sexual union is, it is not enough to ensure a functional marriage. Sex is important and a benefit of marriage, but it is not the glue that holds a marriage together.

Eventually, couples will learn they cannot live on sex alone. Marriage requires understanding, decision making, setting and carrying out goals, encouragement, support, and occasional confrontation. Life happens. There are bills to pay, financial decisions to make, and children to rear. Everyday living requires clear communication. The degree of skill with which you communicate helps or hurts your marriage.

Good communication is critical if you want to function as one. It promotes understanding, a sense of security, clarity, and trust. Plus, good communication gets necessary things done. Additionally, your marriage is enhanced, and your children are much more emotionally secure when you learn to communicate well.

The primary function of communication is to transfer information. You communicate for many different reasons. For example, you can use it to entertain, persuade, inform, deceive, encourage, comfort, propagandize, or educate. Like many of God's gifts, the ability to communicate is neither good nor evil but serves the purpose of the user.

In chapter twelve, I suggest several ways you can use your words to demonstrate your love for others. I have also reminded you that your heart is the source from which your words flow. What you say and how you say it to your spouse can build trust and understanding or undermine them.

It is difficult to overstate how critical communication is to the health of your marriage. It is an essential tool you use for building the trust and understanding necessary for the oneness God wants for you. If you are genuinely committed to the health of your marriage, you must also commit to communicating effectively to realize the loving relationship which is possible for you.

Good communication involves a sender and a receiver of information. Since I have dealt rather thoroughly with listening in chapter twelve, I want to focus on the other side of communication: sending the message. Being an effective messenger is necessary to your goal of becoming one with your spouse. It is my opinion that many couples fail to understand the importance of effective messaging and the potential for good in their relationship. The lack of attention to this part of communication is unfortunate and causes lots of misunderstandings, frustration, and unnecessary conflicts. Your words have great power, and you need to take care and learn to be purposeful and proactive in how you use them.

The fact that your words can help or hurt someone you love is a good reason to examine your heart. What is in your heart concerning your spouse? Do you have a deep commitment to doing what is best for him or her? Do you value them as your equal—a person with feelings, needs, and innate worth? Or do you see them as a means to an end, someone to use to satisfy your needs for security or sex, someone to make you happy? Is there a need to reevaluate or repent for your attitude toward them? Do you need to develop the habit of checking your spirit or calming yourself before you allow your anger to take control?

You must be intentional if you want to build your marriage through your messages. By that, I mean you need to be purposeful and deliberate in your communication. For example, you can commit to making it a habit to encourage, support, and respect your spouse in what you communicate and how you do it. This commitment will require discipline and thoughtfulness. If you are lazy or take your relationship for granted, you will continue to reap what you are sowing. If you want your spouse to know that you care, you will find a way to communicate that.

What would happen in your marriage if you decided to make an encouraging comment or paid a compliment to your spouse every day? Positive, thoughtful messages can gradually change the whole atmosphere of your relationship.

How would you describe the emotional atmosphere of your relationship with your spouse? Is it cold, warm, angry, or friendly? Is it safe to talk? What changes can you make, or what can you do to make it safe to talk? Do you have a critical spirit? Are you generally complaining or negative? Change that by looking for something positive to say about your spouse every day. Try this and watch the change that takes place in your communication.

Confidentiality is another part of creating a safe environment. What you discuss privately is a sacred trust and must remain confidential unless there is explicit permission to share it.

Since communication is such a big deal in marriage, you should be careful about the way you deliver your messages. Speaking clearly and accurately will help you avoid any misunderstandings. Think about what you want to say, and do not expect your spouse to read your mind. Is what you are saying worth being understood? If so, communicate as clearly as possible. Think: What am I trying to say? What do I want you to understand?

Making an effort to communicate implies that your message and your spouse are valuable. Sloppy communication sends a different message. The following ideas may help you give your communication the importance it deserves.

- Think before you speak. What do you want your spouse to understand? Calm down by taking a deep breath, and allow your mind to take control of your words. Be deliberate and precise about what you say.

- Give a clear context to what you are saying. For example, you may want to talk about something you discussed a few hours or days ago. Your spouse may have no clue what you are talking about if you jump right in without giving them context about the subject. Bridge the time gap by saying something similar to "Can we talk again about where we will spend Christmas this year?" Get the idea?

- Remember that your spouse is not a mind reader. Maybe you married the smartest guy or gal in the world, but they cannot read your mind. Stop making this silly assumption, and talk clearly about what you are thinking. Hold yourself responsible, not them, if they fail to know what you are thinking.

Now let's talk about some situations that may be difficult to discuss. All marriages have problems or situations that are a bit awkward but need to be addressed. Building a good marriage is not for the weak. However, doing the tough conversations well will strengthen your trust and understanding and bring you closer to being the "one" God intended you to be. And remember, problems don't fix themselves. Here are some ideas that may help you tackle hard conversations.

- Set a time to talk about the problem when both feel rested. Be deliberate and avoid times when you are tired and less able to control your emotions.

- Take turns listening to each other without interrupting.

- Listen well and attempt to summarize what you heard.

- Focus on the issue, not on fixing your spouse. Take owner-ship as "our problem."

- If you cannot resolve the issue, agree to continue thinking about it, and set another time to talk. Commit to solving the problem together.

- Agree to seek the help of a professional counselor or a wise adviser if you get stuck and cannot resolve the problem.

- Keep a short list of issues. Avoiding problems is toxic to your marriage. Don't let problems build up. Deal with is-sues as they arise so you can focus on the immediate prob-lem and not get drawn into another subject. Resentment and frustration grow if you allow concerns to go unaddressed, and this can contribute to a deterioration of your relation-ship. Facing your problems together is a significant part of building a healthy marriage.

To close this section on communication, I want to recommend an exercise I have used with several couples. I call it the Two-Minute Drill because it is a two-minute communication exercise in talking and listening. You may want to give it a try.

The exercise goes like this. First, you agree on the subject or issue you want to discuss. (I suggest you begin with an issue that is relatively simple and gradually move to the more complicated ones when you have somewhat mastered the exercise.) Next, one of you will talk for two minutes or less about your concerns, feelings, and so on regarding the subject, while the other concentrates on listening. (You will be surprised how long two minutes can be when you are doing this.) The listening partner listens without interrupting and summarizes the essential ideas of what they think they heard. The listener states the facts they have heard without criticism or rebuttal. At this point, the talker responds about whether or not they feel they were heard and clarifies if needed. Next, the listener becomes the talker for two minutes, and the process continues until you resolve the issue or you reach an agreement to continue the discussion at another time.

Try this. You will be surprised at how challenging but effective it can be.

Creative Conflict

I love peace and harmony. I want everything to be calm and peaceful. I don't like conflict, especially with my wife, but I have learned that conflict is normal. Believe it or not, conflict can be good. People who learn to use conflict well will tell you it can help achieve the sense of "oneness" that God intended.

To use conflict to an advantage for your marriage, you need to begin by accepting the fact that disagreements, differences of opinion, and perceptions of reality are normal in marriage. To believe that these differences should disappear because "we love each other" is pure fantasy.

While healthy marriages have essential areas such as faith in common, there are many possibilities of potential conflict within that marriage. Why is this so? First, men and women think differently. There is scientific evidence that our brains process information differently. Women tend to be more emotional in their processing, while men lean more to the logical side. We may be considering the same issue but come at it from two different points of view. Blame that on our brains.

Another reason you have conflict is related to your family of origin. The roles your parents played and how you expressed feelings and celebrated birthdays and holidays have conditioned your expectations about how you should do these things. When you married, you brought expectations and experiences of two families into your family. Working through these differences can be quite challenging. If you have come from vastly different backgrounds, you will likely face more adjustments than those from similar backgrounds. However, it is very likely you can achieve the oneness you desire if you choose to build on your strengths and respectfully accept your differences.

Becoming one doesn't mean you need to think alike and agree on everything. On the contrary, healthy marriages are built by two independent people who choose to become interdependent to honor God and each other. God's grace and your commitment to become one will enable you to grow strong as you work through your conflicts and vicissitudes of married life.

Let's face it; life can be hard at times. To live well, you must learn to solve problems from the time you are young until you take your bow as the curtain closes. The more important the relationship, the more critical it becomes to work through conflicts. The most important relationship we have is with our spouse.

Some areas of conflict will be rather simple to resolve, while others may take a long time and require much more commitment and hard work. I believe the first step to making your conflicts work for the good of your marriage begins with a paradigm shift. You will need to stop thinking conflict is inherently wrong and that problems will somehow go away if you avoid them. You will need to take some common-sense steps to use conflict to move you closer to the goal of becoming one. Consider how you can use the following ideas to navigate your disputes effectively.

Before you can solve a problem, you must recognize a problem exists. This can be difficult if there is the underlying fantasy that people who love each other don't have problems. All marriages have problems to resolve. But some folks don't want to admit their marriage is not perfect. Somehow, they perceive that people who love each other ought to always think the same, feel the same, and agree on everything. That is not realistic of any relationship that has much depth to it.

It should concern you if you never have arguments or disagreements because if you don't, your marriage is being dominated by one of you, or you are too afraid to approach the subject that concerns you. I'm not saying you should look for an argument to prove you are normal. I'm saying that you should acknowledge and address issues when they do arise. You can build a healthy marriage by facing and resolving problems together.

Learn to address dysfunctions that give rise to your conflict. You create conflicts when you do something that crosses boundaries, disappoints, or breaks agreements or understandings. For example, one of the significant issues of many couples is how they manage money. You need to address the problem when one of you disregards your agreements about the budget. Choosing not to deal with an issue of this importance has led to very serious financial and marital trouble for many couples.

Very likely, there is an underlying issue to such conflicts that needs resolution. Power, insecurity, selfishness, or lack of respect for agreements could be the motivation behind the dispute over money. You may never know, and this will never get resolved unless you address it. Use the conflict to help you build a strong relationship of trust and understanding, which will bless you and bring honor to God.

Next, approach the issue with the expectation and intention of something good coming from your discussion about it.

Merriam-Webster defines *conflict* as "a clash between hostile or opposing elements, ideas, or forces." This definition makes conflict sound like war, and it may have felt like a war in some heated encounters with your spouse.

If your disputes become a war of wills where there are a winner and a loser, you may win the battle, but your marriage will be the loser. On the other hand, if you avoid conflict at all costs, you don't get essential issues resolved, and this leads to surface talk and a lack of emotional intimacy. Either way, your marriage is the loser. So you need to learn to think differently about conflict. It does have a significant upside if you will learn how to handle it effectively.

How can your marriage be improved by handling conflict well? There are several ways in which resolving conflicts can strengthen your marriage. Anytime you work out a solution to an issue, you combine your energies and thinking to accomplish the task. You experience oneness when you think, pray, and work together to deal with an issue. Working through a conflict demonstrates that you can solve problems if you commit to working together. The more you do this, the more you become part of one team.

Some conflicts can be challenging to resolve, but doing so builds confidence and trust in each other and strengthens the very foundation of your relationship. You get the sense that "I'm not in this alone. I have a partner who will help."

Not only does resolving conflict build your marriage relationship, it also helps you grow individually. To solve a dispute, you will need to learn to listen well and think about the concerns of your spouse. Stephen Covey uses the idea of "Think Win, Win" when trying to resolve a conflict. How can each of us get what we need by finding a solution satisfactory to both of us? The key to this is to agree about the essential issue and make necessary adjustments or compromises without giving up on the core concern. This approach causes you to think deeply and unselfishly and commit to helping both of you to win as long as you come to an acceptable solution to the conflict.

One other word on using conflict to build your marriage is necessary. Learn to see disagreements as "our" problem, no matter which one of you acted poorly. Let's go back to the issue of money and see how this idea can play out. You have some choices about how to deal with a money issue with your spouse: ignore it, blame them for the problem, or treat it as "our" problem.

While being angry and disappointed with their actions are justified and natural, you need to think about how you may have contributed to the issue and what you can do to help. Don't misunderstand; each person is responsible for their decisions. However, you may have helped create an environment that contributed to their behavior. For example, you may have developed a budget without any input from them. Or you may have unrealistic expectations about how much you need for specific expenses. The point is to be open to discussing how you can be understanding and helpful in resolving the problem. Your marriage wins or loses by how you approach the issue. Make adjustments, and offer whatever help you can. Seek help from experts on the subject and professional counseling if warranted. Remember, it is "our" problem, not yours alone.

INVESTMENT REVIEW

1. In what ways do you think your marriage is part of God's plan for your personal growth?

2. Do you agree or disagree with the following statement? *The goal of having a "functional" marriage is more biblical and realistic than a "happy" marriage.*

3. What are three significant areas that are critical in developing a functional marriage? What is the basic idea behind each of these areas?

4. Why is it important that your marriage be a top priority in the way you invest your time and energy? Where do you need to work more intentionally?

CHAPTER FOURTEEN

Preparing Your Child for Life

Children are a gift of the Lord; the fruit of the womb is a reward.
—Psalm 127:3

The birth of your child changes your life forever. Along with this wonderful gift come the privilege and responsibility of guiding the new life that has been entrusted to you. What you do for this child will influence him for his entire life. And just as your life is a time-sensitive trust from God, your child is entrusted to you for a brief period of training. You have only a few years to prepare him for life. You must pay attention to what matters most and be proactive in how you deal with this awesome responsibility.

The Cultural Challenge

One of the major challenges Christian parents face is the tension between the value system of our culture and that of the kingdom of God. While there are some beneficial aspects of our current culture, its primary concerns have to do with temporary things such as wealth, popularity, beauty, and fame. To ignore the negative effects of our culture will be to sell out to materialism and rear your children with a shallow worldview that is subject to loss and disappointment.

The kingdom's eternal values are concerned with our relationship with God and building a godly character. As a citizen of the eternal kingdom, our time on earth is to be invested in becoming more like Christ and expressing his care for the growth and well-being of our spouse and children.

As we have seen in our discussion of Matthew 22:36–40, the primary concern of life is our relationships. Those who dare to travel this road do so by faith in God. We can't see God, but we trust him to guide us by his Spirit and the teachings of the Bible. By faith, we are "saved" from our selfishness and are continually growing to be like Christ. It is through his example and the indwelling of his Spirit that we learn how to love God above all else and to love others as we learn to love ourselves.

Earlier chapters addressed some ways you can love people in general. The last chapter was devoted to how to develop a loving oneness with your spouse. Now let's give attention to loving your children well, living out the Christ-life in your relationship with them.

How Do You Define Success?

Do you want your child to be successful in life? Of course you do. But how do you define success? Do you use the standards of heaven or the world to guide your child?

A significant challenge in Christian parenting is to deal with the reality that the world defines success one way, and God defines it another. It is your responsibility to choose the value system you will emphasize in parenting your child. While there are many practical things your child will need to learn about living in the temporal world, there are also eternal values he will need to guide him in making choices related to the issues he deals with every day. How you define success will significantly influence your parenting and the foundational values you attempt to teach your child.

Make no mistake about it; your values affect your children. "More is caught than taught" is an old saying about teaching values to our children. What you say is important, but what you do is what you believe. Children tend to believe what you believe. According to Proverbs 22:6, there is a strong probability that the eternal values you teach your child will have a continuous good effect throughout his life: "Train up a child in the way he should go. Even when he is old he will not depart from it." Since that is true, what will happen if your values are indistinguishable from the cultural values of this world?

Reflect on the maps or ideas about parenting you developed while growing up under the authority of your parents. What maps do you need to keep or discard? You are now the parent, and it is your responsibility to decide how you will raise your children. I've told my adult children to think about how their mother and I dealt with them and discard what was not good and keep that which was helpful. Parenting is more important than your job or your hobbies; it is more consequential than almost anything you will ever do.

With this idea in mind, let's look at some ways you can love your child by embracing eternal values. Assuming your heart and head are in the right place, what are some things you can do to give your child what he needs to understand who God is and grow as he has intended?

Your Child Is a Gift from God

Christian parenting is characterized by the unmistakable certainty that your child is a gift from God. Psalm 127:3 says, "Behold, children are a gift of the Lord; the fruit of the womb is a reward."

What is your attitude about your child? Is he simply the biological product of a sexual relationship between you and your spouse? Is your child an accident? Is your child something that can be disposed of because he is an inconvenience?

Like other areas of faithful living, Christian parenting begins with your agreement with scripture. Your attitude about your child is to be shaped by what God says about them, not by cultural mores. Why does it matter that you strongly believe your child is a gift from God? It matters because it is true and because your attitude will determine how you approach parenting. It also matters because your child tends to value and see himself the way you do. This deep emotional sense of worth is highly influential in what your child will come to believe about himself. Your child deserves to have the personal security and stability that come from knowing she is a beautiful gift from God.

Children need to know they are a gift from God to you. Several years ago, this truth was illustrated in a conversation with my children. Our talk began with an urgent question.

"Are we rich?" One morning, Nathan, about ten, shot that question at me. Kristen, his younger sister, was in earshot of the query and came closer, awaiting my response. I had recently bought a used Mercedes, and I assumed this had sparked Nathan's question. And since I had always encouraged them to ask any question they wanted, I was obligated to answer. I saw this as an excellent teachable moment and decided to use it to talk about what their mother and I considered made us rich.

My response went like this: "We have everything we need to take care of our family. We don't have lots of money, as some people do, but we have enough. But to answer your question, yes, we are rich! Know why? Because your mom and I have the two of you, and that makes us rich." I didn't directly answer his question about the Mercedes, but I think he and Kristen got the message I was trying to convey.

Sometimes children listen well to what you are telling them. A few months after this incident, I had an encounter with Kristen, beautifully illustrating this fact. We were in a discussion about money and possessions when she remarked, "Daddy, we're rich, aren't we? Know why? 'Cause you've got Nathan and me." What a reassuring and touching moment! My beautiful little girl had put into words the thought of her unsurpassed worth to the two most influential people in her life!

The fact that your child is a gift from God is a foundational attitude that will guide you to walk humbly before God. Accepting your child as a gift from God will also inspire the gratitude and sense of responsibility required to love your child well. God made your child and gave her into your care for a little while. It is up to you to use your time and influence with her wisely. Here are some more ways for you to invest in the life of your child.

Bless Your Child with Unconditional Love

I believe many people are confused about what it means to love another person. This confusion can lead parents to "love" their child conditionally. Conditional love creates problems for your child because they are tasked with learning what they need to do to earn your love.

Parents are often confused about how to love their children. I believe much of the confusion about healthy and unhealthy parenting happens because parents do not understand the difference between emotional attachment and parenting love. Let me explain.

Emotional attachment is part of parenting love but can lead to conditional love if the parent is unhealthy. Parents who use their children to meet their personal emotional needs require their children to meet certain conditions in order to receive their love.

Emotional attachment has to do with an emotional bond between you and your child. For the mother, this attachment happens typically during pregnancy. However, there are situations in which the mother is so traumatized, immature, or dysfunctional that she is emotionally unable to attach to her child. Situations like this are potentially very problematic for the child's emotional development.

Fathers generally become attached rather quickly as they hold their children and help attend to their physical needs. Such attachments are vital for the child and form the foundation for the possibility of a healthy love that can prepare the child for life. But just as attachment alone is not enough to make a good marriage, neither is it enough to make for healthy parenting.

I have observed instances in which attachment to a child was unhealthy, served to meet the need of the father or the mother. Somehow the child was seen as completing the parent, fulfilling some unmet emotional need or the balm for some emotional wound. Perhaps the child was to provide the love that was missing in a loveless marriage. Whenever this kind of attachment takes place, the child is objectified and burdened with the unspoken responsibility to meet the emotional need of the parent. This type of situation also makes the parent dependent on the child to supply an emotional need. This creates an atmosphere where the parent's discipline and guidance are based on their need to stay in the good graces of the child. Nothing good comes of this for the child or the parent.

What I have just described is conditional love. It isn't love at all. It is a form of abuse: a kind of relationship where the parent gives the child what he wants if the child will meet the parent's emotional needs. The parent's emotional dependency is a dead-end street. This form of "parenting" happens when the adult is too emotionally immature to act like the adult in the relationship with their child. An emotionally immature parent cannot rear an emotionally healthy child.

What is unconditional love? The word *unconditional* means there are no conditions you place on your child for him to receive your love. Parenting love does not require the child to be beautiful, intelligent, socially adept, able to meet your needs, or respectful to be loved. While those things may make you momentarily happy with your child, you love them just as much when you are displeased with their behavior. There are times when you may not like your child's behavior and have angry or negative feelings about them. However, love causes you to act in their best interest and not on your momentary feelings. This is how parenting love should work. Sounds like the way God loves us, doesn't it?

Your Heavenly Father's unconditional love is the model for you to follow with your children. You don't earn his love by being pretty, smart, kind, or by saying your prayers or doing religious things. God created you in his image, and he continually wants and seeks the very best for you. He provides what you need; he guides and strengthens you in challenging times. He picks you up when you fall, forgives your failures, and encourages you to keep trying. He listens when you talk to him. God holds you responsible for the way you behave, but that in itself is one of the surest signs of his love. He does not play silly games to get you to love him. He loves you whether or not you love him.

Practice Excellent Communication

Smart parents learn how to win their child's heart. Communication is an important key to making this happen. Good communication is vital to establishing and developing an understanding and cooperative relationship with your child. It is one of your best tools to win your child's heart and form the trust and mutual respect necessary for his growth and success. The earlier you begin talking with and listening to your child, the better. If you develop this pattern of speaking and listening early, it will make communication more natural when your adolescent child tends to become more independent. They will know where to turn when they need a trusted person to listen and help them think through difficult decisions.

Since communication is such an essential tool for building a good relationship with your child, doesn't it seem wise to know how to use it with them? Think about that. What do you want your child to think and feel about himself? Do you want to encourage him and build trust? Do you want to know your child and their joys and concerns? What character qualities do you want them to develop? Communication, along with consistent behavior on your part, is a great instrument to accomplish these things.

Most parents will confess we have said things to our children in a moment of anger or disappointment we wish we could take back. It takes a lot of maturity and self-awareness to always use our words well. Sometimes we forget our children have feelings and are affected by what we say and how we say it. When we speak disrespectfully to them, we should hold ourselves accountable and apologize, just as we would hold them responsible for the same kind of thing. We should not dismiss our child's unacceptable behavior, but before we correct them, we should think about how to deal with it without acting badly also. Being the parent doesn't give us the right to use our words destructively.

My personal experience has been that the more I attempted to say positive and encouraging things to my children, the less I had to deal with problems. Negativity doesn't work well. If you expect good behavior, try this: instead of always watching for things to correct, create an environment that is healthy for you and your children. Whenever possible, emphasize the positive, and you will see your child grow in confidence. Your positive approach will also enable them to deal well with the instances when you are disappointed with their behavior and impose corrective measures.

If you practice a noncritical, encouraging manner with your child, you will win his heart and create an environment in which he wants to obey and please you. Speaking to encourage and guide your child will bless you and your child for years to come.

Listening is the second step and is perhaps even more important than the first. Listening is more problematic for most of us because it requires a good deal of discipline and practice. However, the effort to listen well can build a level of trust and cooperation that few other things can. Listening is just another way to say, "I love you so much."

I had high expectations for my young children, and this came across at times as being too demanding. I plead guilty for having expected too much at times. Thankfully, there was the love and openness where my children could talk to me without fear of reprisal. On one occasion, when I was giving Nathan a hard time about something, he gave me this reminder: "Dad, you have to remember, I'm just a little boy." Wow, did that sting! I stopped whatever I was saying and doing and looked into his big blue eyes and said, "Nathan, you are absolutely right, and I am sorry. Thank you for telling me that. I will try to do better." What do you think that exchange did for the relationship?

Your child has feelings and concerns that are important to him. These may seem insignificant and "childish" when compared to your challenges. Of course, he doesn't have bills to pay, cranky people to negotiate with, and the needs of other family members to meet. But be careful that you don't dismiss or minimize his problems. He lives in his child-world of bullying, competition, academic expectations, sibling conflict, and perhaps the stress of adjusting to a divorce or a blended family. He needs you to listen to him at his level, just as you would be expected to attend to an adult you respect. Try to hear and put yourself in his place. Use your imagination to think about how it would be to be in his shoes. Recall situations in your childhood when you had fears and concerns that may relate to what he describes. Even if you don't understand, keep trying, and let him know you are listening and interested in what he has to say.

For more detail on listening to your child, I suggest you refresh your memory by reviewing the communication section in chapter twelve. The basic guidelines in chapter twelve also apply to how you listen to your child.

Encourage Self-Discipline

If your child is to succeed in relationships and their field of work, they must learn to accept responsibility and live accountably with others. One of your most important jobs as a loving parent is to help them develop these character traits. Teaching self-discipline will be a work in progress from their early years until the time they are on their own. How do you help your child develop the traits of responsibility and accountability? You teach responsibility and accountability by encouraging self-discipline from the time they are small until they leave the nest. One of the most telling signs of maturity is that a person can deal with difficult and challenging issues in a way that leads to healthy and productive living—what we want for our children.

Since life is often hard and unpredictable, we want to prepare our children to be able to solve problems. People without self-discipline often do stupid stuff that compounds their current problem and hurts them and others who care about them. One of the best ways to love your child well is to provide the loving, consistent discipline they need to grow into a responsible adult.

Through many years of parenting and attempting to help others in this venture through my counseling practice and conference leading, I have developed what I believe to be a helpful working definition of *discipline*. It goes like this: "Discipline is the process of helping your child to understand how he should act and doing that in such a manner that he will gradually accept your teaching and incorporate it into his life."

The goal is for your child to absorb what you teach and consistently act on it. When he does well without your prompting, your teaching has stuck, and he has become self-disciplined in that area. Discipline is about the present and the future. Good discipline now leads to the potential for your child's good behavior in the future. Let's explore this idea a little further.

My definition assumes you, the parent, are the authority or teacher, and the child is the learner. You are to teach your child, and your child's responsibility is to learn to understand and apply what you are teaching. Some parents get confused about their role as the authority, and that turns the relationship upside down; the child has the unnatural position of being the authority. Your child needs you to assume parental authority in the relationship.

This mistake can take place for different reasons. Parenting is hard work, and some are too lazy to put the necessary time and effort into it. Others are distracted by various concerns and allow their children to fend for themselves. Some parents are willing to put up with any behavior as long as the child is happy. Some parents are merely following the way their parents raised them. They feel it is disrespectful to question anything their parents did or contend, "I turned out all right, and if it was good enough for me, it is good enough for my child."

There are at least two good reasons why you should take your authority with your child seriously. First, God has placed you in that role. God has given this child into your care for a short while, and you are accountable to him for the way you teach your child. Search the scriptures for this concept, and you will see this to be undeniably true.

If scripture is not enough to convince you, think about this in a common-sense way. Although it is not 100 percent true in all cases, most adults have more understanding and wisdom about life than their children. Why? Because you have learned from mistakes you have made or because your reasoning is more mature, and you can see the potential danger of certain actions.

Another important idea is that discipline is a process. We deal with processes every day. If you want to bake a cake, paint a room, or buy a car, you follow some steps or processes to get it done. Discipline is a process because it includes your immediate and long-term goals for your child, the ideas or methods for achieving those goals, and the flexibility to grow with your child and change methods as his needs and maturity dictate.

Think of the process of discipline as a box that can be expanded or retracted as needed. A young child is limited in thinking and experience and therefore needs a small box that allows freedom equal to his ability. As he matures, the box gets bigger; boundaries are expanded to accommodate his new level of maturity. This process continues as your child shows more responsibility in handling your expectations. If a violation takes place, the box shrinks back to where the behavior is until your child proves he is capable of handling more responsibility.

When you think about it, your expectations for your child's behavior become the issue at the center of the process. The kind of person, the character you want your child to develop is the core issue in discipline. It is your awesome privilege and responsibility to guide this process of character development of your child. He desperately needs your help because he is not able or possibly not very interested in charting the course of his moral development. Some institutions and individuals will be glad to take this job for you. Some may even be helpful and supportive, but it is your job to set the expectations for your child and get the process going.

Give your best effort in setting and enforcing reasonable expectations, and as Proverbs 22:6 predicts, "When he is old he will not depart from it."

Think about the kind of person you want your son or daughter to be when they are twenty-five or thirty years old. The expectations you work toward while they are under your care can go a long way toward building the foundation for the character that will bless them and generations to follow. God's primary concern for your development is that you become more like Jesus. What does this imply concerning the person you want your child to become?

What is the key to making these ideas about discipline work well with your child? It's the approach, manner, and attitude with which you guide him. For example, you can have the attitude that "I'm the adult, and you are the child, and you will do as I say," and that may get the behavior you want, but your child may resent you for using your power that way. There are times when it may come down to a power struggle, but think about how much better it will be if you have the approach to win your child's cooperation rather than to force it. While there should be no question about which of you is in charge, it is also important to remember to come across as friendly yet firm. Maintaining a positive relationship while getting the behavior you expect is an integral part of all relationships.

How do you feel if your boss curses you or demeans you? Have you ever had someone correct you who left you feeling respected in the way they did it? If so, you were able to acknowledge your error and want to fix it. That's the parenting manner or attitude I'm attempting to describe.

The long-term goal for your discipline is to help your child internalize your external control. You want to win his heart and help him understand that even the punishment you must use to correct his behavior is because you love him too much to allow him to go uncorrected. The hope is by lovingly dealing with all his behavior, good and unacceptable, you will encourage him to discipline himself and mature to the point he no longer needs you to do it.

Below are several ideas you may find helpful as you attempt to use discipline as a tool with which to love your child. I am indebted to many experts who have helped me think about these concepts and how they apply to proactive guidance for a child. I state these ideas in capsule form with the hope you will be challenged to do some serious thinking and research as you attempt to "train your child in the way he should go":

- You, the parent, are the authority in your home.

- Both parents should commit to developing a disciplined process together and support each other in carrying it out.

- Discipline should recognize the uniqueness of each child and be adjusted accordingly.

- Become a behavior detective and try to understand the cause behind your child's behavior.

- Your child will repeat behavior that you reward.

- Your child will stop behavior that you do not reward.

- Accentuate the positive behavior of your child.

- Use natural consequences of the behavior, and act as soon as possible to connect the consequence to the behavior.

- Use your child's need for approval and their desire to "grow up" to reinforce good behavior.

- Be consistent in the way you deal with your child's behavior.

Work Yourself out of a Job

Effective parenting is a gradual process in which you, the parent, assume less responsibility, and your child takes on more. It is what I refer to as giving your child "roots and wings." Let me explain.

When a child is born, he is dependent on the care of his parents for his very survival. The child is helpless to feed himself or take care of any of his physical needs. Without care, he will die. That is total dependence. However, with basic care for his bodily needs, he will survive.

We see this all the time in the animal world. Every spring, birds find convenient places to nest and hatch their little ones. After a brief period of dependence on nourishment, the babies mature, their wings become strong, and they leave the nest to be on their own. The adult birds have provided safety and food, and the little ones have developed their wings and fly away. It's simple in the bird world.

Leaving the nest should also happen with human children, but it is a little more complicated with us. For one thing, birds don't have the emotional attachment needs we humans do. It seems adult and baby birds instinctively know what they are supposed to do and do it year after year: laying eggs, nesting, hatching, nurturing, and leaving.

We, humans, form necessary emotional attachments between parents and babies, and the growth of strong wings takes a while. Unfortunately, when parents become attached to their children in unhealthy ways, they can't or won't let go, and their babies never grow wings. This unhealthy attachment is not how it should be, and it is a great disservice and an unloving thing to do to a child. Loving your child well means you must balance the dependence and independence needs of your child so they can grow their wings, leave the nest, and become independent of you and assume adult responsibilities in the world.

Balancing the dependence and independence needs of your child means you need to know when to hold on and when to turn loose. It's very similar to helping your child learn to ride a bike. You must risk the possibility of harm as opposed to always protecting the child.

Some parents struggle with the protective instinct and limit their child's development by not turning loose when they need to. This process also involves assessing your child's readiness and skill to do certain things. For example, if your child is beginning to learn to ride a bike, you may need to hold on more until he can acquire the balance and skill he needs. As he becomes more skillful or independent, you will turn loose more and eventually stand aside and admire his ability to be on his own.

Think about this metaphor of learning to ride a bike as you approach different areas of growth and responsibility for your child. Help where there is a legitimate need for help. Teach your child how to do things for himself rather than always doing things for him. Sometimes it is easier to do it yourself, but if you do it, this signals to your child that he is incompetent to do it. It can set a pattern of dependence that you will come to regret later.

As your child grows in his ability to help, he needs to be taught to be a cooperative member of the family. This happens as you teach him to do simple things such as picking up his clothes, brushing his teeth, taking a bath, making his bed, doing his homework, and helping with cleaning and other household chores. Involving your daughter or son in everyday tasks teaches them to participate in family life at the level they are able and develop a growing sense of competence as they approach the time when they get to try out their wings.

Don't misunderstand me to be saying that you need to take all the fun out of their childhood. There needs to be a balance of fun and responsibility. Helping your child develop his wings will prepare him for the transition to young adulthood. Loving your child well requires you to work with the understanding that your child will need to transition from depending on you to a time when he can take care of himself. Do him and yourself a big favor by gradually working yourself out of the job of parenting him.

Summation

Time flies. Before you know it, the baby you held in your arms is in high school. I know, sometimes you think time stands still as you deal with helping your child through difficult times. But time moves on, and soon they are ready to leave home. You only have them under your care and guidance for a few years, compared to their potential life span. And that time is critical for preparing the foundation on which they can build the kind of life that will bless them and honor God.

I have attempted in this chapter to focus on five ideas that will help you love your child in a healthy, genuinely loving way. You see, loving someone is not just about how you feel about them. It is practical. It does what is in the best long-term interest of that person. So the five things I have suggested you consider are as follows:

1. Agree with God that your child is his gift to you. Let that attitude permeate all your dealings with your child.

2. Give your child unconditional love. Attach no conditions whatsoever to always seeking the best for your child.

3. Develop a good relationship with your child by the way you talk with them and by listening to them with your heart.

4. Help your child become increasingly self-disciplined through the loving guidance he needs.

5. Gradually work yourself out of a job by helping your child move from dependency to becoming increasingly independent as they prepare to take on adult responsibilities.

For more detail on these essential parenting ideas, see my book *Parenting with a Purpose.*[1]

INVESTMENT REVIEW

1. How do you define the "success" you want for your child? What parts of your idea of success are influenced by the current culture?

2. How does the truth that your child is a gift from God affect the way you treat her (Ps. 127:3)?

3. In what ways do you show unconditional love to your child?

4. What are some things you will do in the following areas to invest in the character of your child?
   a. Developing your child's independence
   b. Developing your child's communication
   c. Encouraging self-discipline

PART FOUR

Return on Your Investment

CHAPTER FIFTEEN

Rewards, Present and Future

*Lay up for yourselves treasures in heaven, where neither
moth and rust destroys, and where thieves do not break
in or steal; for where your treasure is, there will your
heart be also.*
—Matthew 6:20–21

Have you invested time or money in something or someone knowing you were foolishly throwing your investment away? Would
you put your money into a stock, real estate, or business without
expecting an acceptable benefit or return on your investment? Wise
investors have learned to weigh the cost against the potential return
on their investment.

Up to this point in the book, I have been challenging you to
invest your life in the plan God has for you. I have laid out my case
with the understanding you have a choice to make about following
Jesus and his teachings. Furthermore, I believe this choice is, by far,
the most crucial one you will ever make—one that will determine
your character and personal destiny.

Embedded in all that I have said to this point is the biblical teaching of reward for righteous living and punishment for snubbing God's plan. I have hinted at the idea of reward or return on investment throughout the book. Now I want to be more explicit about your reward or return on investing in God, yourself, and others. Let's begin by answering a question that troubles some people.

Is Being Rewarded for Serving God a Biblical Idea?

I want you to consider this question: "What's in this for me?" "Are you kidding me?" you may ask. "Who would think about personal gain from following Christ?" On the surface, that does seem unspiritual, doesn't it? However, receiving a reward for being faithful to God is a prominent concept in Jesus's teaching. Take a few minutes to read his words in the Sermon on the Mount in Matthew 5–7, and you will be amazed at the number of times he offers a reward for our faithful service.

I must admit that I am turned off by the idea of using Christ and his sacrifice for personal financial gain, but that is not what I'm getting at in this chapter. What I have gained is more valuable than any amount of money. When I accepted Christ as my Savior, I gained eternal life and heaven. What he accomplished through his death and resurrection is my gain! I needed and wanted what he alone could provide for me, and there was nothing I could do to earn it. His sacrificial death makes forgiveness free to all who will accept him through faith.

Dr. David Jeremiah has this to say to those who are troubled by the idea of rewards for serving Christ:

> Some people say we should not be lured into goodness by promises of a bonus, for goodness has its reward. While that argument sounds logical and moral, it is entirely out of harmony with what the

Bible teaches. The Bible never defends the concept of rewards; rather, the idea is accepted as if it is the most natural and normal thing for us to expect.[1]

There is a beautiful passage in Ephesians that serves as a theological foundation concerning how we come to Christ in faith and how we are to do good works after we accept him as our Lord. This text lays the groundwork for answering the question, "What's in it for me?"

> For by grace you have been saved through faith; and that not of yourselves, it is the gift of God; not as a result of works, that no one should boast. For, we are His workmanship, created in Christ Jesus for good works, which God prepared beforehand that we should walk in them (Eph. 2:8–10).

Faith in Jesus determines your salvation and eternal destination. Our works on earth determine our rewards in heaven. Christ has saved us, but our choices determine what is in it for us once we get to heaven. You can become incredibly wealthy in the things that matter most!

Notice in the statement to the Ephesians that we are "created in Christ Jesus for good works." One of the major themes of the book of James is that saving faith produces good works in the believer. Faith in Christ saves us, and good deeds follow. James raises the question about the authenticity of one's profession of faith if he has no works: "What use is it, my brethren, if a man says he has faith, but he has no works? Can that faith save him?" (James 2:14). Indeed, we are saved by faith in Christ, but the kind of faith James is questioning is faith in word or profession only. Head knowledge does not save, and it does not produce good works. James continues his point in verse 18 of the same chapter: "But someone may well say 'you have faith, and I have works; show me your faith without the works, and I will show you my faith by my works.'"

Faith saves us from the power and penalty of our sins. Our faith in Christ saves us from the hell we deserve. Through Christ's work, we get to go to heaven. That is one part of the salvation Christ has made available to us. But there is more. We are saved to serve him with good works while we are here on earth. And those good works will be rewarded in heaven. How marvelous is that! Not only do we get to go to heaven because of Christ's death and resurrection for us, there are rewards we can gain from our work for him during our lifetime!

Maybe you've not paid much attention to this prominent teaching in scripture. Or perhaps you've believed that accepting Jesus and being baptized is the total picture of what it means to be a follower of Jesus. Jesus not only wants you to gain heaven because of what he has done for you; he also wants you to earn rewards now as well as others that will be waiting for you when you get to heaven. There is an excellent ROI for those who live godly lives.

But you may still object: "It just doesn't seem right to want to gain something for doing the things Christ wants us to do." Make no mistake about it; our motive for serving God does determine whether or not God will reward us for what we do. Jesus's teaching about this is obvious. Remember what he says about this in the Sermon on the Mount? "Beware of practicing your righteousness before men to be noticed by them; otherwise you have no reward with your Father who is in heaven" (Matt. 6:1).

The motive of wanting to be praised by other people for good deeds cancels out the reward we might otherwise receive from God. Jesus tells us to call no attention to ourselves. He assures us, "Your Father who sees in secret will repay you" (Matt. 6:6).

Without a doubt, Jesus encourages us to seek rewards. His teachings challenge us to choose the "narrow way" that leads to life over the "broad way" that leads to spiritual death. In Matthew 6:19–20, he instructs us concerning the superior value of heavenly treasure over earthly ones: "Do not lay up for yourselves treasures upon earth, where moth and rust destroy, and where thieves break in and steal. But lay up for yourselves treasures in heaven, where neither moth nor rust destroys, and where thieves do not break in or steal."

While passages such as this clearly say that there will be rewards in heaven, they do not in any way preclude benefits from serving the Lord while we are still on earth. The Psalms and Proverbs encourage us to gain wisdom and experience the blessings of the Lord for everyday living. For example, Psalm 1 says the person who meditates on and lives out the law of the Lord will be like a fruitful tree planted by nourishing waters. However, the unbeliever will not endure but will be like "chaff," which the wind blows away. The Beatitudes and the rest of our Lord's Sermon on the Mount instruct us how to live a blessed life as participants of his kingdom in the present tense.

Everyday Rewards for Following Jesus

We are mistaken to think our reward for living for Jesus is only in the future. While there will be rewards in heaven, we have many rewards or gifts as we follow Jesus every day. Jesus said in John 10:10, "I came that they might have life, and have it more abundantly." Was he speaking only of the future, or was he also indicating the life he offers is the best thing going in the here and now? The gospels picture him as caring about the current circumstances of people as he healed the sick, fed the multitudes, gave sight to the blind, restored the health of the crippled, cleansed lepers, broke the bondage of those possessed by demons, associated with "sinners," and forgave the sins of those who believed in Him.

Jesus gives you an abundant life now as well as when you get to heaven. If you have "invested" your faith in him, there are many returns on that investment that you need to be aware of and appreciate every day. What are some of the daily benefits of serving Christ?

- You are forgiven of your sins now, and you have become a child of God. You are born again from a life of darkness and ultimate destruction to a life that is secure in Christ. God has made you a new creation in Christ, and the old patterns of selfishness, sin, and bondage will pass away as you continually choose to obey him.

- You have the Holy Spirit, the Spirit of Jesus, living in you to guide you and help you grow into the image of Christ. The Spirit will lead you into truth and will comfort you in sorrow and guide you in how to make decisions that are critical for doing God's will for your life.

- You have the Bible, God's written word, to guide you to know God intimately and to instruct you in the way to deal with specific situations and principles for everyday living. The ethical standards of the Ten Commandments, the Sermon on the Mount, Jesus's many parables and teachings, and the whole of the New Testament are without parallel among other religious systems. In other words, to follow the way of Christ is to be challenged to live abundantly as his Spirit works in you to bring you toward maturity.

- As a Christian, you get to live your life for something and Someone greater than yourself. What you do matters in the larger scheme of life. Your words, time, and money make a difference. You get to join Christ in his work to bring the world to himself. As Paul wrote in 1 Corinthians 3:9, "We are God's fellow-workers." You may think your role is insignificant, but you have the opportunity to influence your family, neighbors, and friends for Christ by the way you invest your time, energies, money, and gifts.

- You have the assurance that God will sustain you and grow you through painful life experiences. As believers, we are not immune to life's difficulties and tragedies. God doesn't put his children in a protective bubble. However, he gives us something the nonbeliever does not have. "What is that?" you ask. He promises he will be present to bring something good from the difficulty we are facing. Paul, a Christ-follower, wrote in Romans 8:28: "And we know that God causes all things to work together for good to those who love God, to those who are called according to His purpose." Like you and other believers, I have had some tremendous storms in my life, and God has honored this promise and brought good out of potential tragedy. Life is hard, but God is able and willing to help you in times of need.

- You have the incredible privilege of prayer and the promise that God will honor any prayer you pray if it is according to his will. It is mind boggling to realize that you can communicate with the awesome Creator of this vast universe! Through prayer, you can confess your sins and receive forgiveness. You can ask for guidance for all situations you face and praise God for his goodness and daily benefits. In prayer, you can petition him for the needs and concerns of others and pour out your heart to him in times of hurt and profound sorrow. Through prayer, you keep connected with God, your source of knowledge and strength for living an abundant life.

- Among the many rewards for living the Christian life is the encouragement and support you receive from others who share your commitment to him. It is wonderful to have family members, neighbors, church members, and work associates who know Christ intimately and confront the same kinds of issues that come from living in a culture that does not support your worldview. Among these believers, you can build and maintain trusting friendships and rely on their wisdom and help when needed. Very few things in life are more valuable than a Christian friend.

- Allowing Christ's love to guide your relationships with your spouse and children can build loving and supportive bonds that nothing can emulate this side of heaven. There is nothing better on earth than a healthy, loving Christian family.

- As believers, we have a hope that is exclusively ours. The world's idea of hope is not grounded in the reality of who Christ is but is a "feeling" that good things may happen. As a believer, your belief in Christ is the guarantee or assurance that what God has begun in you he will complete. He has saved you, is continuing to keep you, and will perfect his saving work when you stand before the Father in heaven, justified by Christ's death, burial, and resurrection.

This hope is an awesome gift when you consider the reality of death. The life of Christ, which comes into us on our profession of faith in him, is unbroken by your physical death because it is his life, eternal life, within you. And you can face the temporary losses of your dearest Christian loved ones and friends because God will keep his promise, just as he has done throughout your life. Sadly, this is something the unbeliever does not have. There is a very thrilling and reassuring word about this in Paul's first letter to the Thessalonians:

> But we do not want you to be uninformed, brethren, about those who are asleep, that you may not grieve, as do the rest who have no hope. For if we believe that Jesus died and rose again, even so, God will bring with Him those who have fallen asleep in Jesus...Therefore, comfort one another with these words (1 Thess. 4:13–14, 18).

Wow! If all this is not enough, you get to be with Jesus when you die and spend eternity with him. How great is your reward for serving him!

Rewards in Heaven for Following Jesus

I believe it is fair to say that most of us don't spend much time thinking about heaven. We are so busy and caught up in the hectic pace of our life on earth that we don't live with the awareness that there is another world to which we are going. For the follower of Christ, that world is called heaven. Hell, the opposite of heaven, will be the world of those who refuse to accept Christ.

What we know about heaven comes from the Bible. Heaven itself is a wonderful reward for those who put their trust in Jesus. Heaven is a real place, just as New York, London, and Paris are real places. But the beauty of heaven far exceeds that of the most beautiful place on earth! In the Revelation, John describes heaven as having walls built of precious stones and streets paved with gold! Imagine that. Gold, a precious metal on earth, is used for pavement in heaven!

The ruler of heaven is God, the Lord and Creator of the universe. There is no crime, injustice, sickness, sorrow, or death there. The heroes of faith, such as Abraham, Moses, Joshua, Joseph, and Paul are there. Your faithful loved ones and friends will welcome you there also! And, of course, your Lord Jesus is there waiting for you.

Don't worry about boredom in heaven. There will be nothing boring about being there. We will be busy exploring the breathtaking glory of the place Jesus has gone to prepare for us and doing the fulfilling work our Father will assign to us. And for endless ages, we will live in a heavenly body in the presence of Jesus.

In addition to all the blessings of being in heaven, we will receive the rewards we have sent ahead while living faithfully on earth. In his book *The Law of Rewards*, Randy Alcorn makes this observation about laying up treasures: "Jesus didn't tell us not to store up treasures. On the contrary, he commanded us to store up treasures. He said, 'Stop storing them up in the wrong place, and start storing them up in the right place.'"[2] Alcorn further states that Jesus isn't saying it's wrong to invest but that we should be cautious to make a smart investment, not a stupid one.

A careful study of Jesus's parables and the entirety of his teachings will lead you to the conclusion that he wants us to become incredibly wealthy in the things that matter most in life. Your Savior wants you to live the abundant life now and to receive great rewards in heaven as well!

What should motivate us to follow the teachings of Christ? We serve him because we love him. Jesus said, "If you love me you will keep my commandments" (John 14:15). Rewards in heaven come as we demonstrate our love for Christ by being obedient.

God has created us to want to be winners. We don't invest our money or time with the idea or desire to waste either of them. Christ wants us to get heavenly rewards because he loves us. He wants the best for us, just as we want the best for our spouse, children, or friends.

I am not describing a "prosperity gospel." Serving Jesus is a smart investment of your time, talents, and possessions. What I'm saying is true for the wealthy and the poorest among us. I believe that many who have less in this world's treasures will have the greatest rewards in heaven. God's great interest is not in your earthly wealth but your character. He wants you to be the kind of person who recognizes that heaven's currency is a kind of wealth you can gain by your obedience to Christ. That currency is beneficial on earth and will provide rewards in heaven.

It is wise to remember that you are responsible to God for all he has given you. Being responsible implies accountability on your part. Paul reminds you of this sobering truth in Romans 14:12: "So then each one of us shall give account of himself to God." Think about that. One day, you will stand in judgment before him who sacrificed his only Son to save you from the power and penalty of your sin. You will give an account of how you have used your words, influence, time, and possessions.

Yes, there is an accounting day in our future, a day when God will judge believers according to our works. This judgment will not determine whether you go to heaven but will show how well you have used your life and possessions to serve God and others. This judgment is about rewards. So be aware: the decisions you make in this life determine your rewards in heaven.

What are some of the future rewards promised to those believers who intentionally live to obey and honor the Lord? In *Answers to Questions About Heaven*,[3] Dr. Jeremiah identifies five "crowns" that we can receive as rewards.

In the Old Testament, a crown usually signifies an actual head-dress worn by royalty or other persons of high merit or honor. In the New Testament, the term *crown* is often used in a figurative sense, signifying a spiritual reward.[4]

First-century Christians were familiar with the Olympics and other competitive games that were part of the Roman culture. Athletes participating in the races and other events disciplined their bodies and endured rigorous training with one thing in mind: to win the coveted crown. Paul and other New Testament writers use the background of these competitions to challenge believers to pay attention to how we live. We need to give our best effort to finish the race well and receive the reward God will give us. What will God reward? Let's explore the five specific awards God wants to recognize us for on that day.

The Disciplined Life

Corinth was the host city of the Isthmian Games. The following challenge in 1 Corinthians 9:24–27 was not lost on believers who heard and read these words:

> Do you not know that those who run in a race all run, but only one receives the prize? Run in such a way that you may win. And everyone who competes in the games exercises self-control in all things. They then do it to receive a perishable wreath, but we an imperishable. Therefore I run in such a way, as not without aim; I box in such a way, as not beating the air. But I buffet my body and make it my slave, lest possibly, after I have preached to others, I should myself be disqualified.

From reading Paul's letters to the various churches, it appears the Corinthian church, more than any other, was beset with divisions and other issues resulting from their immaturity and lack of personal discipline. What is the reward, the crown, he is challenging them to pursue? Many of them lacked focus and were undisciplined in their conduct. They needed to pursue the rewards that come from a self-disciplined life.

Paul is implying that a crown awaits those whose lives are marked by self-discipline. What does this say to us who live in a culture of luxury and plenty? If we are to receive God's recognition at the judgment, we must bring all areas of our life under the Lordship of Christ. That means we are to dedicate our body, mind, time, money, energies, and talent to serving him. We must stay focused on what it means to love God supremely and to love others as we love ourselves. Living a disciplined life will bring honor to Christ and will reward you with the Father's "Well done" when you stand before him in heaven.

The Witnessing Life

I believe God expects us to witness to others of our faith in him. Jesus calls us "salt and light." He also tells us, "Let your light shine before men that they may see your good works and glorify your father who is in heaven." There are several ways to witness to others. Of course, sharing the gospel as the Spirit leads us is something we should be ready and willing to do as God makes opportunities available to us. We need to always be alert to opportunities to speak of our faith in interactions we have every day. Won't it be wonderful to see people in heaven who are there because you and others cared enough to speak to them about the Lord!

I believe God has a special reward for those who have dedicated themselves to having a witnessing life. I was a young boy when I was saved in a Vacation Bible School. While the pastor gave me the opportunity to accept Jesus, there were several witnessing lives that had prepared me for that decision. And there have been many believers who have taught and encouraged me in the faith through the years. It is encouraging to know that our words of encouragement and our faithful living can be part of leading others to Christ.

In 1 Thessalonians, the tenderness and pride Paul felt for these believers are revealed. Paul spent at least three weeks in Thessalonica on his second missionary journey (Acts 17:1–10). While there, God-fearing Greeks and several prominent women became believers as a result of his witness.

As happened in Philippi and other places, Paul's witness about Jesus as the Messiah to the Thessalonians evoked anger and persecution among some of the Jewish residents. The situation became so heated that the believers got Paul out of town during the night. Reading chapters 1 and 2 leaves the strong impression that these believers had taken their faith seriously. Paul heard of their faithfulness in other towns he visited and was encouraged and very proud of them. So pleased was he that he refers to them as his "crown": "For who is our hope or joy or crown of exultation? Is it not you in the presence of our Lord at his coming? For you are our glory and joy" (1 Thess. 2:19-20).

Be encouraged in knowing that your faithful living and witness in your family, at work, at school, and "chance" encounters can be used to bring others to Christ. Be proactive and use your life and words to encourage others to follow Christ; there will be a crown waiting for you.

The Anticipatory Life

First-century Christians lived with the expectation, the anticipation, of Christ's return in their lifetime. This sense of hope fueled a passion in Paul and others to live with urgency about the gospel. They wanted to be ready in the event Christ should suddenly return.

The passage we are about to look at comes near the end of Paul's life. Christ has not returned, and Paul is in prison, expecting to be executed for his faithfulness to Christ. Look at what he wrote about his situation in 2 Timothy 4:7–8: "I have fought the good fight, I have finished the course, I have kept the faith; in the future there is laid up for me the crown of righteousness, which the Lord, the righteous Judge will award me on that day; and not only to me, but also to all who have loved His appearing."

Here, Paul speaks about a "crown of righteousness" that he and all who love Christ's appearing will receive. What is he saying to us? The fact that Christ had not returned did not cancel Paul's reward. The reward is based on living in anticipation of his return. This is purely a life of working for Christ based on faith. That faith or trust is what saved Paul and kept him anchored to God's promises. Paul's anticipation of meeting Christ encouraged him to finish the race and keep the faith.

I believe Christ is coming to earth again; that may not be before I die. My preference would be that he will return before I die, but it doesn't really matter because I know at some point I'm going to see Jesus. The point is that I need to anticipate meeting him one way or the other. Each day we need to live with the purpose of serving the Lord, knowing that this could be the day he returns or I meet him in death.

The Enduring Life

The New Testament was written during a time of persecution. Many of these letters include encouragement to believers to keep the faith and endure the suffering imposed by the enemies of the church. The Roman Empire was notorious for its cruelty to believers under Nero (AD 54–68). The apostle John, imprisoned on the Isle of Patmos, tells the seven churches of Asia Minor what the "angel of the church" has to say to them. The second message is to believers in Smyrna who are going to be facing persecution. He challenges them to remain faithful, even if doing so costs them their life. A crown awaits those who endure persecution: "Do not fear what you are about to suffer. Behold, the devil is about to cast some of you into prison, that you may be tested, and you will have tribulation ten days. Be faithful until death, and I will give you the crown of life" (Rev. 2:10).

Are you aware that many countries outlaw Christianity today? We have seen some isolated instances of persecution of Christians in our country. There is, I believe, a growing animosity toward evangelical Christians in America as our society seems to be moving further and further away from the biblical principles that undergird our founding documents.

Take a moment, and do a search for "persecution of Christians." You are likely to find a list of countries where there is intense persecution of those who believe in Jesus. Burma, China, Eritrea, India, Iran, Nigeria, North Korea, Pakistan, Russia, Saudi Arabia, Syria, and about thirty-eight other countries are on the list. How far are we away from the outright persecution of Christians in our country?

Someday, you may face an issue or situation in which you are told to compromise your Christian faith or lose your job. What will you do? Or maybe you are tempted to lie or cheat to improve your social status or to get the position you want? What will you do?

Religious persecution takes place when a believer is mistreated because of the fact they are a Christian. Persecution can come because we will not compromise biblical teaching on things such as abortion, sexual orientation, and many of the cultural issues we are dealing with in our society. We need to be careful in our behavior so as not to needlessly cause a fight, but we must have the courage to speak the truth in love. Standing for scriptural principles about what's right and wrong is likely to cost you something. Jesus has a word for those who suffer because of their obedience to Him:

"Blessed are you when men revile you and persecute you, and say all kinds of evil against you falsely, on account of me. Rejoice, and be glad, for your reward in heaven is great, for so they persecuted the prophets who were before you" (Matt. 5:11–12).

The Servant Life

Love is to be the operating currency of all of our relationships. We are to love others as we love ourselves. In other words, we are to serve others by encouraging their personal growth. While this truth applies to all people, there are some to whom we have a particular responsibility. There may be several terms that apply to you: husband, wife, parent, boss, manager, friend, son, daughter, minister, doctor, teacher, or counselor. Each role you "play" is to be marked by an attitude of service.

This passage from 1 Peter 5:1–4 is written to church leaders regarding how they are to "shepherd" the people under their care. Because of their role as spiritual leaders, they have authority over others. Peter cautions them to not use their roles for personal gain or control but for the benefit and growth of those under their care. They are to act like Jesus and use their roles to serve the needs of the people for whom they have responsibility:

> I exhort the elders among you, as your fellow-elder and witness of the sufferings of Christ, and a partaker also of the glory that is to be revealed, shepherd the flock of God among you, not under compulsion, but voluntarily, according to the will of God; and not for sordid gain, but with eagerness; nor yet as lording it over those allotted to your charge, but proving to be examples to the flock. And when the Chief Shepherd appears, you will receive the unfading crown of glory.

I believe the principle of service Peter wrote about to these church leaders is applicable to every believer. Every role of authority or influence you have is an opportunity to serve the needs of others, whether it is your spouse, your children, or those who work under your leadership. The towel and the basin are the way of followers of Jesus. The crown of glory awaits us in heaven!

Your Work in Heaven

Another part of the ROI is that you will have opportunities to serve the Lord in heaven based upon how faithfully you serve him right now. The parable of the talents certainly could imply this, as do other teachings of Jesus. This idea of positions of service in Christ's new kingdom order was alive and well among his disciples. In Matthew 20:20–28, the mother of James and John intercedes for her sons by requesting that they become Jesus's right- and left-hand leaders in his kingdom. Scriptures such as 2 Timothy 2:12, Revelation 5:10 and many others also strongly suggest that heaven will be a place of service and activity.

We won't be floating around on clouds eating dessert all day. There will be work to do in God's kingdom, and I believe we will be given positions according to how we have been faithful in using our earthly opportunities to serve him. Search the scriptures on this. While there may not be a well-defined description of all the jobs and their attendant qualifications, the concept of future reward for current faithful service is unmistakable.

The Best Reward of All

Have there been times when you have experienced peace and joy in the presence of Jesus? There have been periods of trials and testing when I have felt myself being carried by the Lord: carried as a weary, fearful child by his strong and caring Father. As I look back on a time when I was forced to make a career change, I can honestly say that was the most difficult and sweetest time of my life. I was under tremendous pressure to leave a job I had loved and begin an entirely new career. I was in my early fifties with one child in college; the second was in her senior year in high school. The Lord had been preparing me to face the reality of my current work situation. I clearly recall the meeting with my supervisor when I was called on the carpet and given the option to compromise my integrity or else. Two weeks later, I handed in my resignation.

Doing the right thing put me in very difficult circumstances. I sometimes look back with wonderment at how I survived. At some point in the first three or four years, I was working as many as four jobs at one time, but God was faithful. As someone has said, "I trusted like it all depended on God and worked like it all depended on me." When I see the Lord, I want to say to him in person what I have said to him so many times as I think about how he supported and led me during that experience: "Thank you, Lord Jesus, for your wonderful presence and peace at that crucial point in my life."

I have certainly had other experiences of the presence of Jesus in my life. He has been there for me as I've said an earthly goodbye, a "See you later," to my younger brother, my parents, and many close friends. I am aware that his presence sustains me every day and he is preparing me for that day when I see him face to face.

I sincerely believe that I will be united with faithful friends and family members who have preceded me! What a wonderful reunion that will be. I certainly hope there will be some rewards the Father will give me. But the best reward of all is to be with Jesus! As marvelous as all the other benefits of heaven will be, nothing will compare to the presence of Jesus!

Heaven is where Jesus is. And there are some specific words I want Him to say to me. Above all else, I want to hear these words: "Well done, good and faithful servant. Enter into the joy of your

Lord." Then, just as the saints do in Revelation 4:10–11, I will lay any rewards I receive at his feet.

INVESTMENT REVIEW

1. What rewards are you currently getting for serving God?

2. What do you need to do to receive God's rewards here and now?

3. What "heavenly" rewards are you sending ahead to be enjoyed and used when you get to heaven?

Acknowledgments

I am deeply grateful to the countless number of people who have made significant investments in my life. My parents, family members, pastors, teachers, professors, financial advisers, friends, and many writers have encouraged me to think deeply about and live proactively for the things that matter most. From my earliest days until now, I have experienced the reality of what *Heaven's Currency* can do when people around you attempt to do what is in your best interest.

This book, composed in my eighth decade, is a culmination of what I have learned from many caring people. God is the Source of all the good that has come to me through these wonderful folks. I am grateful to him and to those who have been so generous with *Heaven's Currency* in their dealings with me.

About the Author

Cos Davis has spent over fifty years in various ministry roles, attempting to help individuals and families invest their lives in the things that matter most. His work as a pastor, seminary professor, education specialist, manager at a publishing board, and licensed clinical pastoral therapist have put him in touch with the struggles people face in their relationships with God, self, and others.

His writings of more than fifty published articles, six traditionally published books, and five e-books are repositories of the common-sense and biblical wisdom he has gained through his rich and varied experiences.

Cos and Cecelia have been married for over fifty years. They have been blessed with two children, Cos Nathan and Kristen Leigh, and four grandchildren, Anna Katherine and Cos Walker Davis and Steven Alec and Jacob Davis Slack.

Cos is an avid reader and finds great satisfaction in writing about parenting, family, and faith issues in his blogs, books, and articles.

Cos received his BA from Belmont University and his ThM, MRE, EdS, and EdD degrees from New Orleans Baptist Theological Seminary. Additionally, he acquired certification and licensure as a clinical pastoral therapist.

You can find more information about Cos's life, books, and blogs at www.cosdavis.com.

Chapter Notes

Chapter One

1. David Kaiser, "How Today's American Crisis Is Different," *TIME* July 2016, https://time.com/4417672/american-crisis-history/.

2. James W. Fowler, *Faithful Change* (Nashville: Abingdon Press, 1996), 9–11.

Chapter Three

1. Stephen R. Covey, *The 7 Habits of Highly Effective People* (New York: Simon & Schuster, 1990), 18.

2. Ibid., 18.

3. Og Mandino, *The Greatest Salesman in the World*, Part 2 (New York: Bantam Books, 1989), 123.

4. H. Richard Niebuhr, *Christ and Culture,* (New York: Harper and Row, 1951), 2. Niebuhr's treatment of this subject is very thorough, covering centuries of Christian leadership responses to this perplexing issue.

5. Ibid., 32–34.

6. Warren I. Susman, *Culture as History* (New York: Pantheon Books, 1984), xx.

7. Ibid., xxii.

8. Niebuhr, *Christ and Culture*, 37.

9. Lewis Joseph Sherrill (*The Struggle of the Soul*, New York, Macmillan, 1963), 12.

10. Alex McFarland, "Our Abandonment of Moral Law," (*Decision Magazine*, January 2019), 16.

11. Ibid., 17.

12. Randy Alcorn, *The Law of Rewards*, Carol Stream, Ill. (Tyndale, 2003), 3.

13. C. S. Lewis, *The Problem of Pain* (New York: Collier, 1962), 93.

14. M. Scott Peck, *The Road Less Traveled* (New York: Touchstone, 2003), 16–18.

15. Cos Davis, "Character and Pastoral Counseling," (unpublished paper, 1997).

Chapter Four

1. Francis A. Schaeffer, *How Should We Then Live?* (Wheaton, Illinois: Crossway Books, 1975), 19.

2. Neil Anderson, *The Bondage Breaker*, Revised Edition (Eugene, Oregon: Harvest House Publishers, 2019), 48.

Chapter Five

1. David Jeremiah, *1 Minute a Day* (Nashville: Thomas Nelson, 2008), 14. The quote is attributed to English novelist Charles Reade.

2. Robert Frost, *The Road Not Taken* (New York: Henry Holt and Company, 1971), 270.

Chapter Seven

1. Jim Elliot made this notation in his diary while he and four others were attempting to bring the gospel to a dangerous indigenous tribe in Ecuador. All five missionaries were killed by those they were attempting to serve. Elliot was only twenty-eight years old at the time of his death. His wife, Elizabeth, tells the story of the heroic effort of Jim and the four others in her 1957 book *Through Gates of Splendor*.

Chapter Eight

1. Og Mandino, *The Greatest Salesman*, 86.

Chapter Ten

1. J. B. Phillips, *Your God Is Too Small* (New York: Simon and Schuster, 1951).

2. Francis Chan, *Crazy Love* (Colorado Springs: David C. Cook, 2008), 97.

3. Timothy Keller, *Making Sense of God* (New York: Viking Press, 2016), 88–91.

Chapter Eleven

1. C. S. Lewis, *Mere Christianity*, rev. ed. (New York: HarperOne, 2001).

2. Stephen Covey, *The 7 Habits of Highly Effective People*, 287.

3. Editors, *The ABC's of the Human Body* (Pleasantville, NY: The Reader's Digest Association, Inc., 1987), 5.

4. Ibid., 23.

5. John McArthur, "Authority for Truth," *Decision Magazine* (January 2019), 15.

6. Peter Fletcher, *Understanding Your Emotional Problems* (New York: Hart Publishing, 1958).

Chapter Twelve

1. Henry Cloud and John Townsend, *Boundaries* (Grand Rapids: Zondervan, 1992), 32.

2. *Marriage Is What You Make It* can be purchased at my website, cosdavis.com, or at smashwords.com.

3. Saint Francis of Assisi was a Catholic friar and preacher born in Assisi, Italy, in 1182 to a wealthy merchant. After his conversion, he renounced his opulent lifestyle and took the vow of poverty. He died in 1226 while listening to the reading of Psalm 142. He was canonized as a saint in 1228. Francis became the patron saint of Italy.

Chapter Thirteen

1. Cos H. Davis Jr., *Marriage Is What You Make It* (Franklin, TN, 2016). Additional information on the subjects of commitment, communication, and creative conflict in marriage is available in this book.

2. Charles Simmons, in *Quotes That Will Change Your Life*, ed. Russ Kick (San Francisco: Palm Island Press, 2015), 114.

3. Rainer Maria Rilke,in *Quotes That Will Change Your Life*, ed. Russ Kick (San Francisco: Palm Island Press, 2015), 95.

Chapter Fourteen

1. Cos Davis, *Parenting with a Purpose* (Franklin, TN, 2009). The focus of this book is how you can apply Christ's teaching in Matthew 22:34–40 to the important work of rearing your child. Once you understand the ultimate purpose of life, you can begin to guide your child in ways that help

him or her grow in understanding God and becoming the person God has intended him or her to be. This book is available at cosdavis.com or smashwords.com.

Chapter Fifteen

1. David Jeremiah, *Discover Paradise* (Nashville: J. Countryman, 2006), 83.

2. Randy Alcorn, *The Law of Rewards*, 18.

3. David Jeremiah, *Answers to Questions about Heaven* (San Diego: Turning Point, 2013), 104–105.

4. William J. Fallis, "Crown," *Holman Bible Dictionary* (Nashville: Holman Publishers, 1991), 321.

Made in the USA
Coppell, TX
05 April 2022